interchange

FIFTH EDITION

Student's Book

intro A

Jack C. Richards

WITH EBOOK

CAMBRIDGE UNIVERSITY PRESS

CAMBRIDGE
UNIVERSITY PRESS & ASSESSMENT

Shaftesbury Road, Cambridge CB2 8EA, United Kingdom

One Liberty Plaza, 20th Floor, New York, NY 10006, USA

477 Williamstown Road, Port Melbourne, VIC 3207, Australia

314–321, 3rd Floor, Plot 3, Splendor Forum, Jasola District Centre, New Delhi – 110025, India

103 Penang Road, #05–06/07, Visioncrest Commercial, Singapore 238467

Cambridge University Press & Assessment is a department of the University of Cambridge.

We share the University's mission to contribute to society through the pursuit of education, learning and research at the highest international levels of excellence.

www.cambridge.org
Information on this title: www.cambridge.org/9781009040426

First published 1994
Second edition 2000
Third edition 2005
Fourth edition 2013
Fifth edition 2017
Fifth edition update published 2021

20 19 18 17 16 15 14 13 12 11 10

Printed in Great Britain by CPI Group (UK) Ltd, Croydon CR0 4YY

A catalogue record for this publication is available from the British Library

ISBN 978-1-009-04041-9 Intro Student's Book with eBook
ISBN 978-1-009-04042-6 Intro Student's Book A with eBook
ISBN 978-1-009-04043-3 Intro Student's Book B with eBook
ISBN 978-1-009-04055-6 Intro Student's Book with Digital Pack
ISBN 978-1-009-04056-3 Intro Student's Book A with Digital Pack
ISBN 978-1-009-04057-0 Intro Student's Book B with Digital Pack
ISBN 978-1-316-62237-7 Intro Workbook
ISBN 978-1-316-62239-1 Intro Workbook A
ISBN 978-1-316-62240-7 Intro Workbook B
ISBN 978-1-108-40605-5 Intro Teacher's Edition
ISBN 978-1-316-62221-6 Intro Class Audio
ISBN 978-1-009-04058-7 Intro Full Contact with Digital Pack
ISBN 978-1-009-04059-4 Intro Full Contact A with Digital Pack
ISBN 978-1-009-04062-4 Intro Full Contact B with Digital Pack
ISBN 978-1-108-40304-7 Presentation Plus Intro

Additional resources for this publication at cambridgeone.org

Informed by teachers

Teachers from all over the world helped develop *Interchange Fifth Edition*. They looked at everything – from the color of the designs to the topics in the conversations – in order to make sure that this course will work in the classroom. We heard from 1,500 teachers in:

- Surveys
- Focus Groups
- In-Depth Reviews

We appreciate the help and input from everyone. In particular, we'd like to give the following people our special thanks:

Jader Franceschi, **Actúa Idiomas,** Bento Gonçalves, Rio Grande do Sul, Brazil
Juliana Dos Santos Voltan Costa, **Actus Idiomas,** São Paulo, Brazil
Ella Osorio, **Angelo State University,** San Angelo, TX, US
Mary Hunter, **Angelo State University,** San Angelo, TX, US
Mario César González, **Angloamericano de Monterrey, SC,** Monterrey, Mexico
Samantha Shipman, **Auburn High School,** Auburn, AL, US
Linda, **Bernick Language School,** Radford, VA, US
Dave Lowrance, **Bethesda University of California,** Yorba Linda, CA, US
Tajbakhsh Hosseini, **Bezmialem Vakif University,** Istanbul, Turkey
Dilek Gercek, **Bil English,** Izmir, Turkey
erkan kolat, **Biruni University, ELT,** Istanbul, Turkey
Nika Gutkowska, **Bluedata International,** New York, NY, US
Daniel Alcocer Gómez, **Cecati 92,** Guadalupe, Nuevo León, Mexico
Samantha Webb, **Central Middle School,** Milton-Freewater, OR, US
Verónica Salgado, **Centro Anglo Americano,** Cuernavaca, Mexico
Ana Rivadeneira Martínez and Georgia P. de Machuca, **Centro de Educación Continua – Universidad Politécnica del Ecuador,** Quito, Ecuador
Anderson Francisco Guimerães Maia, **Centro Cultural Brasil Estados Unidos,** Belém, Brazil
Rosana Mariano, **Centro Paula Souza,** São Paulo, Brazil
Carlos de la Paz Arroyo, Teresa Noemí Parra Alarcón, Gilberto
Bastida Gaytan, Manuel Esquivel Román, and Rosa Cepeda Tapia, **Centro Universitario Angloamericano,** Cuernavaca, Morelos, Mexico
Antonio Almeida, **CETEC,** Morelos, Mexico
Cinthia Ferreira, **Cinthia Ferreira Languages Services,** Toronto, ON, Canada
Phil Thomas and Sérgio Sanchez, **CLS Canadian Language School,** São Paulo, Brazil
Celia Concannon, **Cochise College,** Nogales, AZ, US
Maria do Carmo Rocha and CAOP English team, **Colégio Arquidiocesano Ouro Preto – Unidade Cônego Paulo Dilascio,** Ouro Preto, Brazil
Kim Rodriguez, **College of Charleston North,** Charleston, SC, US
Jesús Leza Alvarado, **Coparmex English Institute,** Monterrey, Mexico
John Partain, **Cortazar,** Guanajuato, Mexico
Alexander Palencia Navas, **Cursos de Lenguas, Universidad del Atlántico,** Barranquilla, Colombia
Kenneth Johan Gerardo Steenhuisen Cera, Melfi Osvaldo Guzman Triana, and Carlos Alberto Algarín Jiminez, **Cursos de Lenguas Extranjeras Universidad del Atlantico,** Barranquilla, Colombia
Jane P Kerford, **East Los Angeles College,** Pasadena, CA, US
Daniela, **East Village,** Campinas, São Paulo
Rosalva Camacho Orduño, **Easy English for Groups S.A. de C.V.,** Monterrey, Nuevo León, Mexico
Adonis Gimenez Fusetti, **Easy Way Idiomas,** Ibiúna, Brazil
Eileen Thompson, **Edison Community College,** Piqua, OH, US
Ahminne Handeri O.L Froede, **Englishouse escola de idiomas,** Teófilo Otoni, Brazil
Ana Luz Delgado-Izazola, **Escuela Nacional Preparatoria 5, UNAM,** Mexico City, Mexico
Nancy Alarcón Mendoza, **Facultad de Estudios Superiores Zaragoza, UNAM,** Mexico City, Mexico
Marcilio N. Barros, **Fast English USA,** Campinas, São Paulo, Brazil
Greta Douthat, **FCI Ashland,** Ashland, KY, US
Carlos Lizárraga González, **Grupo Educativo Anglo Americano, S.C.,** Mexico City, Mexico
Hugo Fernando Alcántar Valle, **Instituto Politécnico Nacional, Escuela Superior de Comercio y Administración-Unidad Santotomás, Celex Esca Santo Tomás,** Mexico City, Mexico
Sueli Nascimento, **Instituto Superior de Educação do Rio de Janeiro,** Rio de Janeiro, Brazil
Elsa F Monteverde, **International Academic Services,** Miami, FL, US
Laura Anand, **Irvine Adult School,** Irvine, CA, US
Prof. Marli T. Fernandes (principal) and Prof. Dr. Jefferson J. Fernandes (pedagogue), **Jefferson Idiomass,** São Paulo, Brazil
Herman Bartelen, **Kanda Gaigo Gakuin,** Tokyo, Japan
Cassia Silva, **Key Languages,** Key Biscayne, FL, US
Sister Mary Hope, **Kyoto Notre Dame Joshi Gakuin,** Kyoto, Japan
Nate Freedman, **LAL Language Centres,** Boston, MA, US
Richard Janzen, **Langley Secondary School,** Abbotsford, BC, Canada

Christina Abel Gabardo, **Language House,** Campo Largo, Brazil
Ivonne Castro, **Learn English International,** Cali, Colombia
Julio Cesar Maciel Rodrigues, **Liberty Centro de Línguas,** São Paulo, Brazil
Ann Gibson, **Maynard High School,** Maynard, MA, US
Martin Darling, **Meiji Gakuin Daigaku,** Tokyo, Japan
Dax Thomas, **Meiji Gakuin Daigaku,** Yokohama, Kanagawa, Japan
Derya Budak, **Mevlana University,** Konya, Turkey
B Sullivan, **Miami Valley Career Technical Center International Program,** Dayton, OH, US
Julio Velazquez, **Milo Language Center,** Weston, FL, US
Daiane Siqueira da Silva, Luiz Carlos Buontempo, Marlete Avelina de Oliveira Cunha, Marcos Paulo Segatti, Morgana Eveline de Oliveira, Nadia Lia Gino Alo, and Paul Hyde Budgen, **New Interchange-Escola de Idiomas,** São Paulo, Brazil
Patrícia França Furtado da Costa, Juiz de Fora, Brazil
Patricia Servín
Chris Pollard, **North West Regional College SK,** North Battleford, SK, Canada
Olga Amy, **Notre Dame High School,** Red Deer, Canada
Amy Garrett, **Ouachita Baptist University,** Arkadelphia, AR, US
Mervin Curry, **Palm Beach State College,** Boca Raton, FL, US
Julie Barros, **Quality English Studio,** Guarulhos, São Paulo, Brazil
Teodoro González Saldaña and Jesús Monserrrta Mata Franco, **Race Idiomas,** Mexico City, Mexico
Autumn Westphal and Noga La`or, **Rennert International,** New York, NY, US
Antonio Gallo and Javy Palau, **Rigby Idiomas,** Monterrey, Mexico Tatiane Gabriela Sperb do Nascimento, **Right Way,** Igrejinha, Brazil
Mustafa Akgül, **Selahaddin Eyyubi Universitesi,** Diyarbakır, Turkey
James Drury M. Fonseca, **Senac Idiomas Fortaleza,** Fortaleza, Ceara, Brazil
Manoel Fialho S Neto, **Senac – PE,** Recife, Brazil
Jane Imber, **Small World,** Lawrence, KS, US
Tony Torres, **South Texas College,** McAllen, TX, US
Janet Rose, **Tennessee Foreign Language Institute,** College Grove, TN, US
Todd Enslen, **Tohoku University,** Sendai, Miyagi, Japan
Daniel Murray, **Torrance Adult School,** Torrance, CA, US
Juan Manuel Pulido Mendoza, **Universidad del Atlántico,** Barranquilla, Colombia
Juan Carlos Vargas Millán, **Universidad Libre Seccional Cali,** Cali (Valle del Cauca), Colombia
Carmen Cecilia Llanos Ospina, **Universidad Libre Seccional Cali,** Cali, Colombia
Jorge Noriega Zenteno, **Universidad Politécnica del Valle de México,** Estado de México, Mexico
Aimee Natasha Holguin S., **Universidad Politécnica del Valle de México UPVM,** Tultitlàn Estado de México, Mexico
Christian Selene Bernal Barraza, **UPVM Universidad Politécnica del Valle de México,** Ecatepec, Mexico
Lizeth Ramos Acosta**, Universidad Santiago de Cali,** Cali, Colombia
Silvana Dushku, **University of Illinois Champaign,** IL, US
Deirdre McMurtry, **University of Nebraska – Omaha,** Omaha, NE, US
Jason E Mower, **University of Utah,** Salt Lake City, UT, US
Paul Chugg, **Vanguard Taylor Language Institute,** Edmonton, Alberta, Canada
Henry Mulak, **Varsity Tutors,** Los Angeles, CA, US
Shirlei Strucker Calgaro and Hugo Guilherme Karrer, **VIP Centro de Idiomas,** Panambi, Rio Grande do Sul, Brazil
Eleanor Kelly, **Waseda Daigaku Extension Centre,** Tokyo, Japan
Sherry Ashworth, **Wichita State University,** Wichita, KS, US
Laine Bourdene, **William Carey University,** Hattiesburg, MS, US
Serap Aydın, Istanbul, Turkey
Liliana Covino, Guarulhos, Brazil
Yannuarys Jiménez, Barranquilla, Colombia
Juliana Morais Pazzini, Toronto, ON, Canada
Marlon Sanches, Montreal, Canada

Additional content contributed by Kenna Bourke, Inara Couto, Nic Harris, Greg Manin, Ashleigh Martinez, Laura McKenzie, Paul McIntyre, Clara Prado, Lynne Robertson, Mari Vargo, Theo Walker, and Maria Lucia Zaorob.

Classroom Language Teacher instructions

Plan of Intro Book A

Pronunciation/Listening	Writing/Reading	Interchange Activity
Linked sounds Listening for the spelling of names, phone numbers, and email addresses	Writing a list of names, phone numbers, and email addresses	"Celebrity classmates": Introducing yourself to new people PAGE 114
Plural *-s* endings Listening for the locations of objects	Writing the locations of objects	"Find the differences": Comparing two pictures of a room PAGE 115
Syllable stress Listening for countries, cities, and languages; listening to descriptions of people	Writing questions requesting personal information	"Let's talk!": Finding out more about your classmates PAGE 118
The letters *s* and *sh* Listening for descriptions of clothing and colors	Writing questions about what people are wearing	"Celebrity fashions": Describing celebrities' clothing PAGES 116–117
Rising and falling intonation Listening for times of the day; listening to identify people's actions	Writing times of the day "Message Me!": Reading an online chat between two friends	"What's wrong with this picture?": Describing what's wrong with a picture PAGE 119
Third-person singular *-s* endings Listening for activities and days of the week	Writing about your weekly routine "What's Your Schedule Like?": Reading about someone's daily schedule	"Class survey": Finding out more about classmates' habits and routines PAGE 120
Words with *th* Listening to descriptions of homes; listening to people shop for furniture	Writing about your dream home "Unique Hotels": Reading about two interesting hotels	"Find the differences": Comparing two apartments PAGE 121
Reduction of *do* Listening to people describe their jobs	Writing about jobs "Dream Jobs": Reading about two unusual jobs	"The perfect job": Figuring out what job is right for you PAGE 122

1 What's your name?

- Say hello and make introductions
- Say good-bye and exchange contact information

1 CONVERSATION My name is Joshua Brown.

A Listen and practice.

Joshua: Hello. My name is Joshua Brown.
Isabella: Hi. My name is Isabella Martins.
Joshua: It's nice to meet you, Isabella.
Isabella: Nice to meet you, too.
Joshua: I'm sorry. What's your last name again?
Isabella: It's Martins.

First names	Last names
↓	↓
Joshua	Brown
Isabella	Martins

B **PAIR WORK** Introduce yourself to your partner.

2 SNAPSHOT

Listen and practice.

Names and nicknames

Nicholas Hoult

Nicholas (Nick)	Madison (Maddie)	Jennifer (Jen)
Emily (Em)	Joshua (Josh)	Isabella (Izzy)
Michael (Mike)	William (Will)	Elizabeth (Liz)

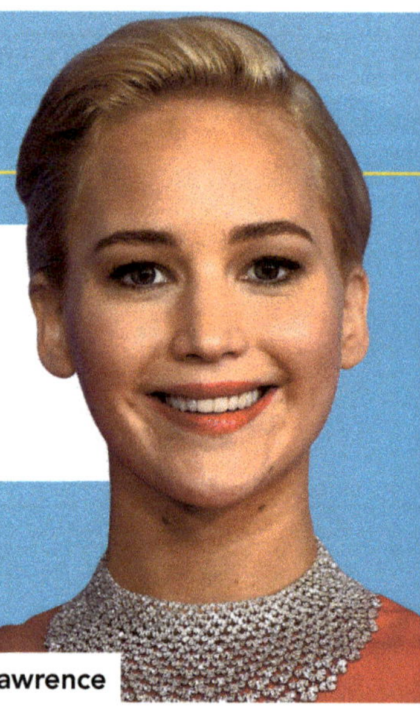

Jennifer Lawrence

What are some popular names and nicknames in your country?
Do you have a nickname? What is it?

3 GRAMMAR FOCUS

My, your, his, her

What's **your** name?	**My** name's Carlos.	What**'s** = What **is**
What's **his** name?	**His** name's Joshua.	
What's **her** name?	**Her** name's Isabella.	

GRAMMAR PLUS *see page 132*

A Complete the conversations. Use *my*, *your*, *his*, or *her*.

1. **A:** Hello. What's ___your___ name?
   B: Hi. ______________ name is Carlos.
   What's ______________ name?
   A: ______________ name is Akina.

2. **A:** What's ______________ name?
   B: ______________ name is Ethan.
   A: And what's ______________ name?
   B: ______________ name is Caroline.

B **PAIR WORK** Practice the conversations with a partner.

4 SPEAKING Spelling names

A Listen and practice.

A	B	C	D	E	F	G	H	I	J	K	L	M	N	O	P	Q	R	S	T	U	V	W	X	Y	Z
a	b	c	d	e	f	g	h	i	j	k	l	m	n	o	p	q	r	s	t	u	v	w	x	y	z

B **CLASS ACTIVITY** Listen and practice. Then practice with your own names. Make a list of your classmates' names.

A: What's your name?
B: My name is Akina Hayashi.
A: Is that A-K-I-N-A?
B: Yes, that's right.
A: How do you spell your last name? H-A-Y-A-S-H-Y?
B: No, it's H-A-Y-A-S-H-I.

My classmates
Akina Hayashi
Ethan Reed

5 LISTENING Your name, please?

How do you spell the names? Listen and check (✓) the correct answers.

1. ☐ Kate ☐ Cate
2. ☐ Erick ☐ Eric
3. ☐ Sophia ☐ Sofia
4. ☐ Zackary ☐ Zachary

6 WORD POWER Titles

A Listen and practice.

Miss Kato (single females)	**Ms.** Yong (single or married females)
Mrs. Jones (married females)	**Mr.** Rodriguez (single or married males)

B Listen and write the titles.

1. ________ Santos **2.** ________ Wilson **3.** ________ Park **4.** ________ Rossi

7 SPEAKING Saying hello

A Listen and practice.

B CLASS ACTIVITY Go around the class. Greet your classmates formally (with titles) and informally (without titles).

8 CONVERSATION Are you Andrea Clark?

A Listen and practice.

Daniel: Excuse me. Are you Andrea Clark?
Sheila: No, I'm not. She's over there.
Daniel: Oh, I'm sorry.

Lena: Matt? This is your book.
Matt: Oh, thank you. You're in my math class, right?
Lena: Yes, I am. I'm Lena Garza.

Jack: Hey, Christy, this is Ben. He's in our history class.
Christy: Hi, Ben.
Ben: Hi, Christy. Nice to meet you.

B **GROUP WORK** Greet a classmate. Then introduce him or her to another classmate.

"Hey, Eduardo, this is . . ."

9 GRAMMAR FOCUS

The verb *be*

I'm	Lena Garza.	**Are you** Andrea Clark?	**I'm** = I am
You're	in my class.	Yes, **I am**. (~~Yes, I'm.~~)	**You're** = You are
She's	over there. (**Andrea is** over there.)	No, **I'm not**.	**He's** = He is
He's	in our class. (**Ben is** in our class.)		**She's** = She is
It's	Garza. (**My last name is** Garza.)	How **are you**?	**It's** = It is
		I'm fine, thanks.	

GRAMMAR PLUS see page 132

A Complete the conversation with the correct words in parentheses. Then practice with a partner.

Ben Hello, Christy. How ___*are*___ (are / is) you?
Christy __________ (I'm / It's) fine, thanks. __________ (I'm / It's) sorry – what's your name again?
Ben __________ (Is / It's) Ben – Ben Durant.
Christy That's right! Ben, this __________ (is / it's) Joshua Brown. __________ (He's / She's) in our history class.
Ben __________ (I'm / It's) nice to meet you.
Joshua Hi, Ben. I think __________ (I'm / you're) in my English class, too.
Ben Oh, right! Yes, I __________ (am / 'm).

B Complete the conversations. Then practice in groups.

Cara	Excuse me. ___Are___ you Alex Lane?
James	No, ________ not. My name ________ James Harris. Alex ________ over there.
Cara	Oh, sorry.

Cara	________ you Alex Lane?
Alex	Yes, I ________.
Cara	Hi. ________ Cara Ruiz.
Alex	Oh, ________ in my history class, right?
Cara	Yes, I ________.
Alex	________ nice to meet you, Cara.

C **CLASS ACTIVITY** Write your name on a piece of paper. Put the papers in a bag. Then take a different paper. Find the other student.

A: Excuse me. Are you Min-ji Cho?
B: No, I'm not. She's over there.
A: Hi. Are you Min-ji Cho?
C: Yes, I am.

10 PRONUNCIATION Linked sounds

Listen and practice. Notice the linked sounds.

I'm Isabella.   She's over there.   You're in my class.

11 SPEAKING Personal information

A Listen and practice.

0	1	2	3	4	5	6	7	8	9	10
zero (oh)	one	two	three	four	five	six	seven	eight	nine	ten

B **PAIR WORK** Practice these phone numbers and email addresses. Then listen and check your answers.

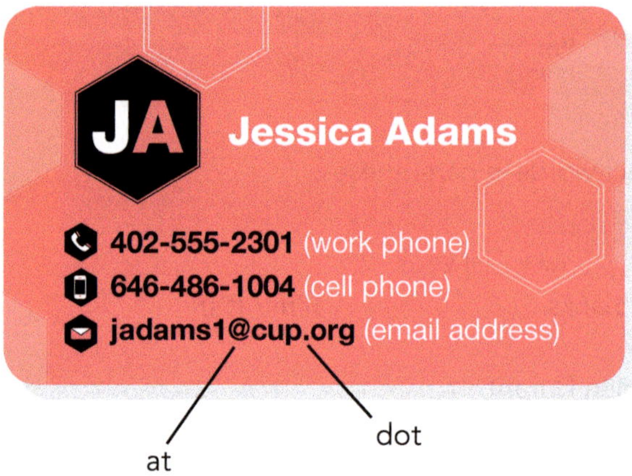

"Her name is Jessica Adams. Her work phone number is four-oh-two, five-five-five, two-three-oh-one. Her cell . . ."

12 LISTENING Contact information

A Isabella and Joshua are making a list of classmates' phone numbers and email addresses. Listen and complete the list.

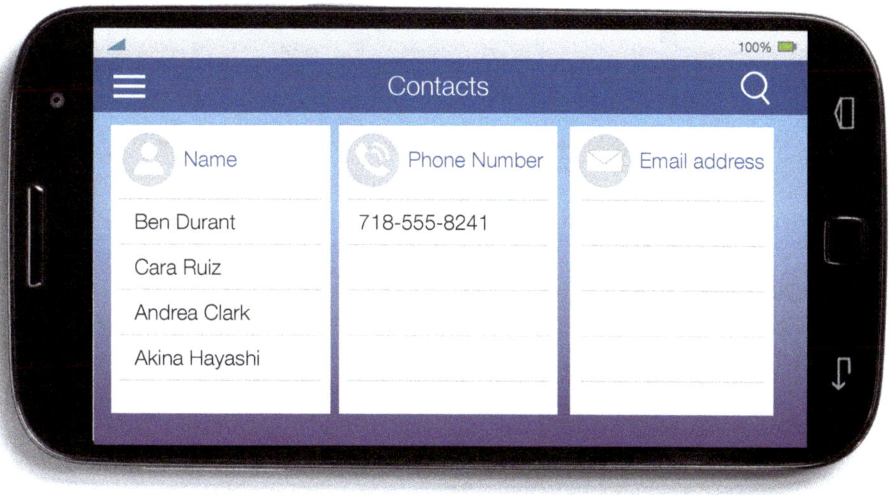

B CLASS ACTIVITY Make a list of your classmates' names, phone numbers, and email addresses.

A: What's your name?
B: I'm Maria Ventura.

A: And what's your phone number?
B: It's 323-555-7392.

13 INTERCHANGE 1 Celebrity classmates

Meet some "famous classmates." Go to Interchange 1 on page 114.

14 SPEAKING Saying good-bye

A Listen and practice.

B CLASS ACTIVITY Go around the room. Say good-bye to your classmates and teacher.

2 Where are my keys?

- Identify and discuss personal and classroom objects
- Discuss the location of items

1 SNAPSHOT

Listen and practice.

Check (✓) the things in your bag.
What is one other thing in your bag?

2 ARTICLES Classroom objects

A Listen. Complete the sentences with *a* or *an*.

articles

an + vowel sound
a + consonant sound

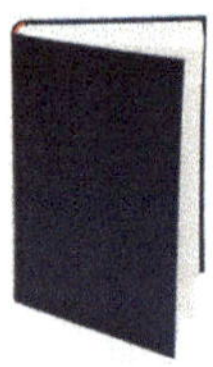

1. This is __________ book.

2. This is __________ English book.

3. This is __________ eraser.

4. This is __________ notebook.

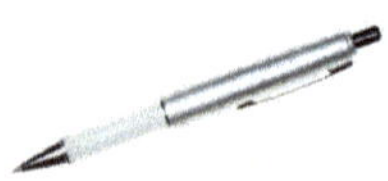

5. This is __________ pen.

6. This is __________ clock.

B PAIR WORK Find and spell these things in your classroom.

backpack	chair	eraser	pen	notebook
board	desk	pencil	wall	wastebasket
poster	door	outlet	book	window

A: This is a chair.
B: How do you spell *chair*?
A: C-H-A-I-R.

3 CONVERSATION What are these?

Listen and practice.

Brandon: Excuse me. What are these?

Christina: They're flash drives.

Brandon: Oh, they're cool. And what's this?

Christina: It's a tablet.

Brandon: A tablet? Really? Wow! It's great!

Christina: Yes, it is. It's a new model.

Brandon: Huh . . . and what's this?

Christina: It's a tablet case.

Brandon: Oh. It's . . . interesting . . . and different.

4 PRONUNCIATION Plural –s endings

A Listen and practice. Notice the pronunciation of the plural **–s** endings.

s = /z/		**s** = /s/		**(e)s** = /ɪz/	
flash drive	flash drive**s**	desk	desk**s**	tablet case	tablet case**s**
cell phone	cell phone**s**	laptop	laptop**s**	class	class**es**
pencil	pencil**s**	backpack	backpack**s**	hairbrush	hairbrush**es**

B Say the plural form of these nouns. Then complete the chart.

phone case

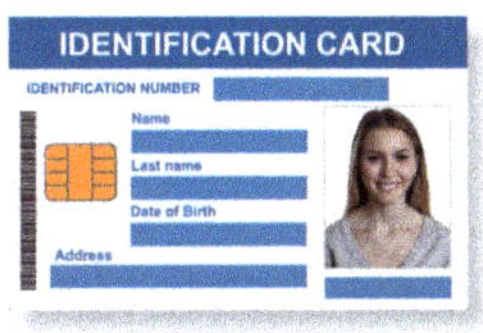

student ID

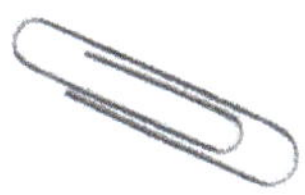
paper clip

newspaper

purse

tablet

television

ticket

box

/z/	/s/	/ɪz/
		phone cases

C Listen and check your answers.

5 GRAMMAR FOCUS

This/these, it/they; plurals

This is a laptop.

What**'s this**?
It's a flash drive.

These are laptop**s**.

What **are these**?
They're flash drive**s**.

It**'s** = It is
They**'re** = They are

GRAMMAR PLUS *see page 133*

Complete these conversations. Then practice with a partner.

1. A: What ___are these___?
B: ______________________.

2. A: What ______________________?
B: ______________________.

3. A: What ______________________?
B: ______________________.

4. A: What ______________________?
B: ______________________.

5. A: What ______________________?
B: ______________________.

6. A: What ______________________?
B: ______________________.

6 SPEAKING What's this called?

A Listen and practice.

A: What's this called in English?
B: I don't know.
C: It's a credit card.
A: How do you spell that?
C: C-R-E-D-I-T C-A-R-D.

A: What are these called in English?
B: I think they're called headphones.
A: How do you spell that?
B: H-E-A-D-P-H-O-N-E-S.

B GROUP WORK Choose four things. Put them on a desk.
Then ask about the name and spelling of each thing.

7 CONVERSATION Where are my car keys?

Listen and practice.

Lauren: Oh, no! Where are my car keys?

Matt: I don't know. Are they in your purse?

Lauren: No, they're not.

Matt: Maybe they're on the table in the restaurant.

Server: Excuse me. Are these your keys?

Lauren: Yes, they are. Thank you!

Server: You're welcome. And is this your wallet?

Lauren: Hmm. No, it's not. Where's your wallet, Matthew?

Matt: It's in my pocket. . . . Wait a minute! That *is* my wallet!

8 GRAMMAR FOCUS

Yes/No and *where* questions with *be*

Is this your wallet?	**Where's** your wallet?
Yes, **it is**. / No, **it's not**.	**It's** in my pocket.
Are these your keys?	**Where are** my keys?
Yes, **they are**. / No, **they're not**.	**They're** on the table.

GRAMMAR PLUS *see page 133*

A Complete these conversations. Then practice with a partner.

1. **A:** ____Is____ this your cell phone?
   B: No, ________ not.
   A: ________ these your car keys?
   B: Yes, ________ are. Thanks!

2. **A:** Where ________ my glasses?
   B: Are ________ your glasses?
   A: No, they're ________.
   B: Look! ________ they in your pocket?
   A: Yes, ________. Thanks!

3. **A:** Where ________ your headphones?
   B: ________ on the table.
   A: No, ________ not. They're *my* headphones!
   B: You're right. My headphones ________ in my backpack.

4. **A:** ________ this my umbrella?
   B: No, ________ not. It's my umbrella.
   A: Sorry. ________ is my umbrella?
   B: ________ on your chair.
   A: Oh, you're right!

B GROUP WORK Choose one of your things and put it in a bag. Then choose something from the bag that is not your object. Find the owner of this object.

A: Is this your pen, Akiko?
B: No, it's not.

C: Are these your keys, Marcos?
D: Let me see. Yes, they are.

9 WORD POWER Prepositions; article *the*

A Listen and practice.

Where is **the** cell phone?
The cell phone is in **the** box.

in

in front of

behind

on

next to

under

B Complete these sentences. Then listen and check your answers.

1. The books are in the backpack.

2. The flash drives are ________________.

3. The newspaper is ________________.

4. The chair is ________________.

5. The wallet is ________________.

6. The glasses are ________________.

C PAIR WORK Ask and answer questions about the pictures in part B.

A: Where are the books? **B:** They're in the backpack.

10 LISTENING Emily's things

Listen. Where are Emily's things? Check (✓) the correct locations.

1. sunglasses	☐ on the table	☐ in her purse
2. ID	☐ in her wallet	☐ in front of the clock
3. headphones	☐ on the chair	☐ next to the television
4. tablet	☐ on the table	☐ under the table

11 SPEAKING Where are Kevin's things?

PAIR WORK Help Kevin find his things. Ask and answer questions.

cell phone   **hairbrush**   **laptop**   **umbrella**   **glasses**   **keys**   **tablet**   **credit card**

A: Where's his cell phone?
B: It's under the chair.

12 INTERCHANGE 2 Find the differences

Compare two pictures of a room. Go to Interchange 2 on page 115.

Units 1–2 Progress check

SELF-ASSESSMENT

How well can you do these things? Check (✓) the boxes.

I can . . .	Very well	OK	A little
Introduce myself and other people (Ex. 1)	☐	☐	☐
Say hello and good-bye (Ex. 1)	☐	☐	☐
Exchange contact information (Ex. 2)	☐	☐	☐
Understand names for everyday objects and possessions (Ex. 3)	☐	☐	☐
Ask and answer questions about where things are (Ex. 4, 5)	☐	☐	☐

1 SPEAKING How are you?

A Complete the conversation. Use the sentences and questions in the box.

Francisco *Hi. How are you?*
Nicole I'm fine, thanks. ______________________
Francisco Pretty good, thanks. ______________________
Nicole And I'm Nicole White.
Francisco ______________________
Nicole Nice to meet you, too. ______________________
Francisco Yes, I am.
Nicole ______________________
Francisco See you in class.

> My name is Francisco Diaz.
> Oh, are you in my English class?
> How about you?
> ✓ Hi. How are you?
> It's nice to meet you, Nicole.
> Well, have a good day.

B PAIR WORK Practice the conversation from part A. Use your own information. Then introduce your partner to a classmate.

"Monica, this is my friend. His name is Kenta. . . ."

2 SPEAKING Is your phone number . . . ?

CLASS ACTIVITY Write your phone number on a piece of paper. Then put the papers in a bag. Take a different paper and find the owner. Write his or her name on the paper.

A: Kamal, is your phone number 781-555-1532?
B: No, it's not. Sorry!
A: Bruna, is your . . . ?

3 LISTENING What's this? What are these?

Listen to the conversations. Number the pictures from 1 to 6.

☐ ☐ ☐ ☐ ☐ ☐

4 SPEAKING What's wrong with this room?

A What's wrong with this room? Make a list. Find 10 things.

B **PAIR WORK** Ask and answer *Where* questions about the picture.

A: Where's the chair?
B: It's on the desk.

5 SPEAKING Yes or No game

Write five yes/no questions about the picture in Exercise 4. Make three questions with "yes" answers and two questions with "no" answers. Then ask a partner the questions.

A: Is the chair behind the clock?
B: No, it isn't.

A: Is the clock in front of the television?
B: Yes, it is.

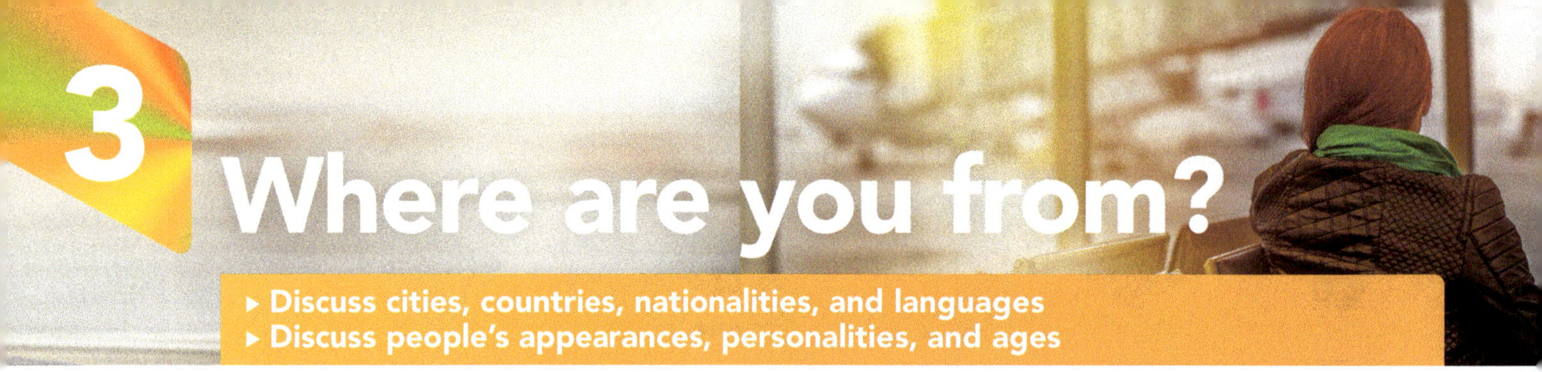

3 Where are you from?

- Discuss cities, countries, nationalities, and languages
- Discuss people's appearances, personalities, and ages

1 SNAPSHOT

Listen and practice.

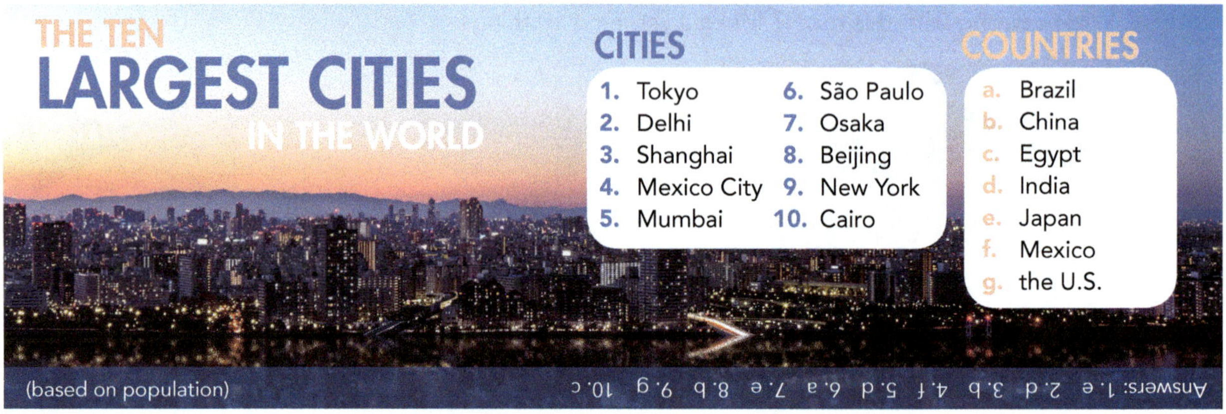

THE TEN LARGEST CITIES IN THE WORLD

CITIES		COUNTRIES
1. Tokyo	6. São Paulo	a. Brazil
2. Delhi	7. Osaka	b. China
3. Shanghai	8. Beijing	c. Egypt
4. Mexico City	9. New York	d. India
5. Mumbai	10. Cairo	e. Japan
		f. Mexico
		g. the U.S.

(based on population)

Answers: 1. e 2. d 3. b 4. f 5. d 6. a 7. e 8. b 9. g 10. c

Match the cities with the countries. Then check your answers at the bottom of the Snapshot.
What other large cities are in each country? What large cities are in your country?

2 CONVERSATION Are you from Rio?

A Listen and practice.

Alexis: Are you from Florida, Felipe?

Felipe: Well, my family is in Florida now, but we're from Brazil originally.

Alexis: Really? My father is Brazilian – from Rio de Janeiro!

Felipe: So, is your first language Portuguese?

Alexis: No, it's English. Are you from Rio?

Felipe: No, we're not. We're from São Paulo.

B Listen to Alexis and Felipe talk to Fernando, Nanami, and Sophia. Check (✓) True or False.

	True	False
1. Fernando is from Spain.	☐	☐
2. Nanami is from Japan.	☐	☐
3. Sophia's first language is French.	☐	☐

3 GRAMMAR FOCUS

Negative statements and yes/no questions with *be*

I'm not	from Rio.	**Are you**	from São Paulo?		I **am.**		**I'm not.**
You're not	late.	**Am I**	early?		**you are.**		**you're not.**
She's not	from Japan.	**Is she**	from the U.S.?		**she is.**		**she's not.**
He's not	from Chile.	**Is he**	from Mexico?	Yes,	**he is.**	No,	**he's not.**
It's not	English.	**Is it**	French?		**it is.**		**it's not.**
We're not	from China.	**Are you**	from South Korea?		**we are.**		**we're not.**
You're not	early.	**Are we**	late?		**you are.**		**you're not.**
They're not	in India.	**Are they**	in Egypt?		**they are.**		**they're not.**

We**'re** = we are

GRAMMAR PLUS *see page 134*

For a list of countries, nationalities, and languages, see the appendix at the back of the book.

A Complete the conversations. Then practice with a partner.

Bogotá, Colombia

1. **A:** ____Are____ Diana and Mario from Ecuador?
   B: No, __________ not. __________ from Mexico.
   A: __________ you from Mexico, too?
   B: No, __________ not . I'm from Colombia.
   A: So, __________ your first language Spanish?
   B: Yes, it __________.
2. **A:** __________ Meera from England?
   B: No, __________ not. She's from Australia.
   A: __________ she from Sydney?
   B: Yes, she __________. But her parents are from India.
   __________ not from Australia originally.
   A: __________ Meera's first language Hindi?
   B: No, __________ not. __________ English.
3. **A:** Ji-hye, __________ you and Kwang-ho from South Korea?
   B: Yes, we __________.
   A: And __________ from Seoul?
   B: No, __________ not. __________ from Busan.

Busan, South Korea

B Match the questions with the answers. Then practice with a partner.

1. Are Liam and Grace from England? __d__
2. Is your first language Mandarin? _____
3. Are you Egyptian? _____
4. Is Mr. Lau from Beijing? _____
5. Is your mother from the U.K.? _____

a. No, he's not. He's from Shanghai.
b. Yes, she is. She's from London.
c. No, it's not. It's Cantonese.
d. No, they're not. They're from New Zealand.
e. Yes, we are. We're from Cairo.

C **PAIR WORK** Write five questions about your classmates. Then ask and answer your questions with a partner.

4 PRONUNCIATION Syllable stress

A Listen and practice. Notice the syllable stress.

China	Brazil	Canada	Malaysia
Turkey	Japan	Mexico	Morocco

B What is the syllable stress in these words? Add the words to the chart in part A. Then listen and check.

English	Spanish	Arabic	Korean
Mexican	Honduras	Chinese	Peru

C **GROUP WORK** Are the words in part A countries, nationalities, or languages? Make a chart and add more words.

Countries	Nationalities	Languages
Brazil	Brazilian	Portuguese
Mexico	Mexican	Spanish

5 SPEAKING Is Bruno Mars from Italy?

A Where are these people from? Check (✓) your guesses.

Bruno Mars
- ☐ Italy
- ☐ the Philippines
- ☐ the U.S.

Morena Baccarin
- ☐ Argentina
- ☐ Brazil
- ☐ the U.S.

Gael García Bernal
- ☐ Brazil
- ☐ Mexico
- ☐ Spain

Mao Asada
- ☐ China
- ☐ Japan
- ☐ South Korea

Chris Hemsworth
- ☐ Australia
- ☐ Canada
- ☐ England

B **PAIR WORK** Compare your guesses. Then check your answers at the bottom of the page.

A: Is Bruno Mars from Italy?
B: No, he's not.
A: Is he from the Philippines?

Answers: 1. the U.S. 2. Brazil 3. Mexico 4. Japan 5. Australia

6 CONVERSATION Who's that?

A Listen and practice.

Nadia Who's that?
Ben She's my sister.
Nadia She's really pretty. What's her name?
Ben Madison. We call her Maddie.
Nadia Madison . . . that's a beautiful name. How old is she?
Ben She's twenty-eight.
Nadia And what's she like? Is she nice?
Ben Well, she's shy, but she's really kind.
Nadia And who's that little girl?
Ben That's her daughter Mia. She's six years old.
Nadia She's cute!
Ben Yes, she is – and she's very smart, too.

7 SPEAKING Numbers and ages

A Listen and practice.

11 eleven	**21** twenty-one	**40** forty
12 twelve	**22** twenty-two	**50** fifty
13 thirteen	**23** twenty-three	**60** sixty
14 fourteen	**24** twenty-four	**70** seventy
15 fifteen	**25** twenty-five	**80** eighty
16 sixteen	**26** twenty-six	**90** ninety
17 seventeen	**27** twenty-seven	**100** one hundred
18 eighteen	**28** twenty-eight	**101** one hundred (and) one
19 nineteen	**29** twenty-nine	**102** one hundred (and) two
20 twenty	**30** thirty	**103** one hundred (and) three

B Listen and practice. Notice the word stress.

thirteen – thirty   fourteen – forty   fifteen – fifty   sixteen – sixty

C PAIR WORK Look at the people in Ben's family for one minute. How old are they? Close your books and tell your partner.

A. Carol – 76

B. Richard – 50

C. Karen – 49

D. Amber – 17

E. Jay and Joe – 10

8 GRAMMAR FOCUS

Wh-questions with *be*

What's your name?	**Who's that?**	**Who are they?**
My name is Sophia.	She's my sister.	They're my classmates.
Where are you from?	**How old is she?**	**Where are they from?**
I'm from Canada.	She's twenty-eight.	They're from San Francisco.
How are you today?	**What's she like?**	**What's San Francisco like?**
I'm fine, thanks.	She's very nice.	It's very beautiful.
	Who**'s** = Who **is**	

GRAMMAR PLUS *see page 134*

A Complete the conversations with Wh-questions. Then practice with a partner.

1. **A:** Look! *Who's that* ?
   B: Oh, she's a new student.
   A: ______________________________?
   B: I think her name is Yoo-jin.
   A: Yoo-jin? ______________________________?
   B: She's from South Korea.
2. **A:** Hi, Brittany. ______________________________?
   B: I'm fine, thanks. My friend Leandro is here this week – from Argentina.
   A: Oh, cool. ______________________________?
   B: He's really friendly.
   A: ______________________________?
   B: He's twenty-five years old.
3. **A:** Azra, ______________________________?
   B: I'm from Turkey. From Ankara.
   A: ______________________________?
   B: Well, Ankara is the capital of Turkey. It's very old.
   A: ______________________________?
   B: My last name is Ganim.
4. **A:** Good morning, Luke.
   ______________________________?
   B: I'm great, thanks.
   A: Cool. ______________________________?
   B: They're my friends from school.
   A: ______________________________?
   B: They're from Miami, like me.

B **PAIR WORK** Write six Wh-questions about your partner and six Wh-questions about your partner's best friend. Then ask and answer the questions.

Your partner	*Your partner's best friend*
Where are you from?	*Who's your best friend?*

9 WORD POWER Describing people

A Listen and practice.

a. pretty
b. handsome
c. good-looking
d. talkative
e. friendly
f. kind
g. funny
h. quiet
i. serious
j. shy
k. short
l. tall
m. heavy
n. thin

B PAIR WORK Complete the chart with words from part A. Add two more words to each list. Then describe your personality and appearance to a partner.

Personality			Appearance		
talkative			pretty		

"I'm tall, friendly, and very talkative."

10 LISTENING Wow! Who's that?

Listen to three descriptions. Check (✓) the two correct words for each description.

1. Nora is . . .	2. Taylor is . . .	3. Austin is . . .
☐ tall	☐ funny	☐ short
☐ pretty	☐ pretty	☐ serious
☐ quiet	☐ handsome	☐ talkative
☐ talkative	☐ serious	☐ tall

11 INTERCHANGE 3 Let's talk!

Talk to your classmates. Go to Interchange 3 on page 118.

4 Is this coat yours?

- Discuss work and free-time clothes; colors
- Discuss the weather and what people are wearing

1 WORD POWER Clothes

A Listen and practice.

B Complete the chart with words from part A.

Clothes for warm weather	Clothes for cold weather
 86°F | 30°C	 32°F | 0°C
______	______
______	______
______	______
______	______
______	______

C **PAIR WORK** Look around the classroom. What clothes do you see? Tell a partner.

"I see jeans, a sweater, boots, and . . ."

2 SPEAKING Colors

A Listen and practice.

white	light gray	gray
dark gray	beige	light brown
brown	dark brown	black

B **GROUP WORK** Ask about favorite colors.

A: What are your favorite colors?
B: My favorite colors are orange and dark blue.

C **GROUP WORK** Describe the clothes in Exercise 1.

A: The suit is black.
B: The socks are dark blue.

3 PRONUNCIATION The letters *s* and *sh*

A Listen and practice. Notice the pronunciation of **s** and ***sh***.

suit	**s**ocks	**s**wimsuit
shirt	**sh**orts	**sh**oes

B Read the sentences. Pay attention to the pronunciation of **s** and ***sh***.

1. This is Jo**sh**ua's new **s**uit.
2. These are **S**arah's purple **sh**oes!
3. Where are my **sh**oes and **socks**?
4. My **sh**orts and T-**sh**irts are blue!

4 CONVERSATION Whose jeans are these?

Listen and practice.

Ashley Great! Our clothes are dry.

Jessica Hey, where is my new blouse?

Ashley What color is your blouse? Is this yours?

Jessica No, this blouse is blue. Mine is white. Wait! It *is* mine. My white blouse is . . . blue!

Ashley Oh, no! Look. It's a disaster! *All* our clothes are blue . . .

Jessica Here's the problem. It's these blue jeans. Whose jeans are these? Are they yours?

Ashley Uh, yes, they're mine. Sorry.

5 GRAMMAR FOCUS

Possessives

Adjectives		Pronouns		Names	
	my		**mine.**	**Jack's** tie.	s = /s/
	your		**yours.**	**Taylor's** shoes.	s = /z/
These are	**his** shoes.	These shoes are	**his.**	**Alex's** coat.	s = /ɪz/
	her		**hers.**		
	our		**ours.**	**Whose** tie is this? It's **Greg's.**	
	their		**theirs.**	**Whose** shoes are these? They're **Taylor's.**	

GRAMMAR PLUS *see page 135*

A Complete the conversations with the correct words in parentheses. Then practice with a partner.

1. **A:** This isn't ___my___ (my / mine) raincoat. Is it ________ (your / yours)?
   B: No, it's not ________ (my / mine). Ask Emma. Maybe it's ________ (her / hers).
2. **A:** Hey! These aren't ________ (our / ours) sneakers!
   B: You're right. ________ (Our / Ours) are over there.
3. **A:** Are these ________ (your / yours) gloves, Erin?
   B: No, they're not ________ (my / mine). Maybe they are Logan's. ________ (His / Your) gloves are gray.
4. **A:** ________ (Whose / Yours) T-shirts are these? Are they Hayley's and Brad's?
   B: No, they're not ________ (their / theirs) T-shirts. ________ (Their / Theirs) are white, not blue.

B **CLASS ACTIVITY** Put one of your things in a box. Then choose a different thing from the box. Go around the class and find the owner.

A: Laura, are these sunglasses yours?
B: No, they're not mine. Maybe they're Joon-ho's.
C: Wei, is this your pen?
D: Yes, it is.

6 LISTENING Her sneakers are purple.

A Listen to someone describe six people. Number the pictures from 1 to 6 in the order you hear them.

☐ Alicia

☐ 1 Sarah

☐ Andrea

☐ Amanda

☐ Cody

☐ Kyle

B **PAIR WORK** Now talk about the people. What colors are their clothes?

A: What color is Alicia's jacket?
B: It's beige.

7 SNAPSHOT

Listen and practice.

What season is it now in your town or city? What's the weather like today?
What's your favorite season?

8 CONVERSATION Are you wearing your gloves?

Listen and practice.

Ashley Oh, no!

Jessica What's the matter?

Ashley It's snowing! Wow, it's so cold and windy!

Jessica Are you wearing your gloves?

Ashley No, I'm not. They're at home.

Jessica What about your scarf?

Ashley It's at home, too.

Jessica Well, you're wearing your coat.

Ashley But my coat isn't very warm. And I'm not wearing boots!

Jessica OK. Let's take a taxi.

Ashley Good idea!

9 GRAMMAR FOCUS

Present continuous statements; conjunctions

I**'m**	I**'m not**	OR:	
You**'re**	You**'re not**	You **aren't**	
She**'s wearing shoes.**	She**'s not**	She **isn't wearing boots.**	
We**'re**	We**'re not**	We **aren't**	
They**'re**	They**'re not**	They **aren't**	
It**'s snowing.**	It**'s not**	It **isn't raining.**	

Conjunctions

It's snowing, **and** it's windy.
It's sunny, **but** it's cold.
It's windy, **so** it's very cold.

GRAMMAR PLUS *see page 135*

A Complete these sentences from a travel show on TV. Then compare with a partner.

1

My name is Dylan Jones. I *'m wearing* ______ a new gray suit. I ______ new black shoes, too. It's raining, but I ______ ______ a raincoat.

2

It's very hot and sunny today. Michael ______ light blue shorts and white sneakers. He ______ a white T-shirt, but he ______ a cap.

3

Adriana Fuentes is from Mexico. She ______ a pretty yellow dress and a brown belt. She ______ high heels and a light brown jacket, but she ______ a coat. Wow, it's really windy!

4

Hee-sun and Kun-woo are here with me today. They're 10 years old. It's really cold, so they ______ winter clothes. They ______ boots, gloves, hats, and scarves. And they ______ heavy coats!

Present continuous yes/no questions

Are you **wearing** gloves?	Yes, I **am**.	No, I**'m not**.
Is she **wearing** boots?	Yes, she **is**.	No, she**'s not**./No, she **isn't**.
Are they **wearing** sunglasses?	Yes, they **are**.	No, they**'re not**./No, they **aren't**.

GRAMMAR PLUS see page 135

B PAIR WORK Ask and answer these questions about the people in part A.

1. Is Dylan wearing a gray suit?
2. Is he wearing a raincoat?
3. Is he wearing black shoes?
4. Is Michael wearing jeans?
5. Is he wearing a T-shirt?
6. Is he wearing a cap?
7. Is Adriana wearing a skirt?
8. Is she wearing a jacket?
9. Is she wearing high heels?
10. Are Hee-sun and Kun-woo wearing swimsuits?
11. Are they wearing gloves and hats?
12. Are they wearing sneakers?

A: Is Dylan wearing a gray suit?
B: Yes, he is. Is he wearing a raincoat?
A: No, he's not. OR No, he isn't.

adjective + noun

My suit is **black**.
I'm wearing **a black suit**.

C Write four more questions about the people in part A. Then ask a partner the questions.

10 LISTENING You look great in pink.

A Listen. What are their names? Write the names **Brittany**, **Ryan**, **John**, **Robert**, **Kayla**, and **Amber** in the correct boxes.

B GROUP WORK Ask questions about the people in the picture.

A: Is John wearing a brown jacket?
B: Yes, he is.
C: Is he wearing a cap?

C GROUP WORK Write five questions about your classmates. Then ask and answer the questions.

Are Maria and Bruno wearing jeans?
Is Bruno wearing a red shirt?

11 INTERCHANGE 4 Celebrity fashions

What are your favorite celebrities wearing? Go to Interchange 4 on pages 116–117.

Units 3–4 Progress check

SELF-ASSESSMENT

How well can you do these things? Check (✓) the boxes.

I can . . .	Very well	OK	A little
Ask and answer questions about countries of origin, nationalities, and languages (Ex. 1)	☐	☐	☐
Understand descriptions of people (Ex. 2)	☐	☐	☐
Ask and answer questions about people's appearance and personality (Ex. 2, 5)	☐	☐	☐
Ask and answer questions about people's possessions (Ex. 3)	☐	☐	☐
Talk and write about my and other people's favorite things (Ex. 4)	☐	☐	☐
Ask and answer questions about what people are wearing (Ex. 5)	☐	☐	☐

1 SPEAKING Interview with my classmates

Match the questions with the answers. Then ask and answer the questions with a partner. Answer with your own information.

1. Are you from Argentina? __h__
2. Where are you and your family from? _____
3. What is your hometown like? _____
4. Is English your first language? _____
5. Who is your best friend? _____
6. How old is your best friend? _____
7. Is our teacher from the U.S.? _____
8. Are our classmates friendly? _____

a. It's very beautiful.
b. Yes, she is.
c. We're from Montevideo.
d. My best friend is Takuya.
e. Yes, they are.
f. No, it's not. It's Spanish.
g. He's nineteen.
h. No, I'm not. I'm from Uruguay.

2 LISTENING Where's your friend Jacob?

A Listen to four conversations. Check (✓) the correct description for each person. You will check more than one adjective.

1. Jacob	2. Monica	3. Hannah	4. Ki-nam
☐ tall	☐ tall	☐ thin	☐ tall
☐ short	☐ talkative	☐ short	☐ short
☐ funny	☐ pretty	☐ quiet	☐ funny
☐ serious	☐ shy	☐ shy	☐ friendly
☐ nice	☐ nice	☐ serious	☐ talkative
☐ shy	☐ friendly	☐ funny	☐ quiet

B Write five yes/no questions about the people in part A. Then ask a partner the questions.

Is Jacob tall?
Is Monica thin?

3 SPEAKING Are these your clothes?

CLASS ACTIVITY Draw three pictures of clothes on different pieces of paper. Then put the papers in a bag. Take three different papers, go around the class, and find the owners.

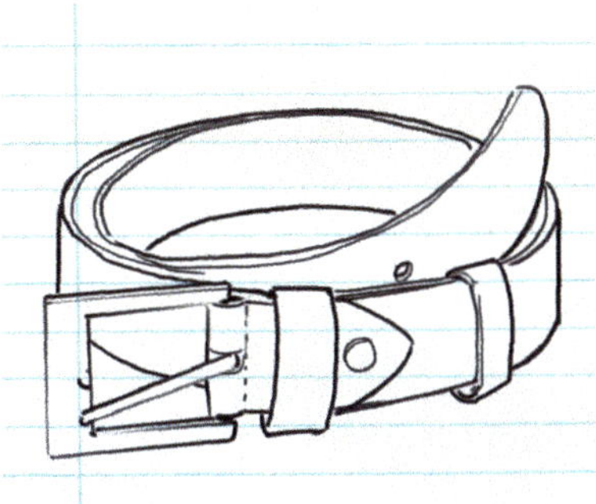

A: Anna, is this your belt?
B: No, it's not mine. Maybe it's Miki's.

A: Ji-hun, are these your sneakers?
C: Yes, they're mine. Thanks!

4 SPEAKING Similar or different?

A Write your favorite things in the chart. Then ask a partner about his or her favorite things. Write them in the chart.

Favorite	Me	My partner
1. season		
2. color		
3. clothes		

B Compare answers. What's the same? What's different? Write sentences.

Spring is my favorite season, and it's Mariana's favorite season. That's the same.
My favorite color is green, but Mariana's favorite color is red, so that's different.

5 SPEAKING I'm thinking of . . .

GROUP WORK Think of a student in the class. Your classmates ask yes/no questions to guess the student.

A: I'm thinking of a student in this class.
B: Is it a woman?
A: Yes, it is.
C: Is she short?
A: No, she isn't.
D: Is she wearing blue jeans?

WHAT'S NEXT?

Look at your Self-assessment again. Do you need to review anything?

5 What time is it?

- Discuss cities and time zones
- Discuss people's activities

1 SNAPSHOT

Listen and practice.

Time Zones

Mexico City 10:00 A.M. | New York 11:00 A.M. | Dubai 7:00 P.M. | Seoul 12:00 A.M.

Is your city or town in the same time zone as one of these cities?
What other events or shows are on television in different time zones?

2 CONVERSATION It's two o'clock in the morning!

A Listen and practice.

Amar: Hello?

Brian: Hi, Amar! This is Brian. I'm calling from New York.

Amar: Brian? Wait. . . . Where are you?

Brian: I'm home on vacation, remember? I'm calling about the soccer game. Great game!

Amar: Oh, that's good. But what time is it there?

Brian: It's 2:00 P.M. And it's two o'clock in Australia, too. Right?

Amar: That's right – it's two o'clock in the morning!

Brian: 2:00 A.M.? Oh, of course! I'm really sorry.

Amar: That's OK. Congratulations on the game!

2:00 A.M. ▼

2:00 P.M. ▲

3 GRAMMAR FOCUS

What time is it?

It's two **o'clock**.

It's two-oh-five.
It's five **after** two.

It's two-fifteen.
It's **a quarter after** two.

It's two-thirty.

It's two-forty.
It's twenty **to** three.

It's two forty-five.
It's **a quarter to** three.

GRAMMAR PLUS see page 136

A PAIR WORK Look at these clocks. What time is it?

1 

2 

3 

4 

5 

6 

A: What time is it?
B: It's ten after ten. OR It's ten-ten.

Is it A.M. or P.M.?

It's six (o'clock) **in the morning**.
It's 6:00 A.M.

It's twelve (o'clock).
It's 12:00 P.M.
It's **noon**.

It's four (o'clock) **in the afternoon**.
It's 4:00 P.M.

It's six (o'clock) **in the evening**.
It's 6:00 P.M.

It's nine (o'clock) **at night**.
It's 9:00 P.M.

It's twelve (o'clock) **at night**.
It's 12:00 A.M.
It's midnight.

GRAMMAR PLUS see page 136

B PAIR WORK Say each time a different way.

1. It's eight o'clock in the morning. *"It's 8:00 A.M."*
2. It's three o'clock in the afternoon.
3. It's six o'clock in the evening.
4. It's twelve o'clock at night.
5. It's 10:00 A.M.
6. It's 4:00 P.M.
7. It's 7:00 P.M.
8. It's 12:00 P.M.

4 LISTENING What time is it in Tokyo?

A Lauren and John are calling friends in different parts of the world. Listen. What time is it in these cities?

City	Time
Vancouver	4:00 P.M.
Bangkok	
London	
Tokyo	
São Paulo	

B Listen again. Check (✓) the correct answers.

1. Tanawat is . . .	☐ getting married.	☐ in São Paulo.	☐ sleeping.
2. Richard is . . .	☐ in London.	☐ in Bangkok.	☐ late.
3. Misaki is . . .	☐ in Tokyo.	☐ in Vancouver.	☐ watching TV.

5 CONVERSATION What are you doing?

Listen and practice.

JAY Hey, Kate!

KATE What are you doing?

JAY I'm cooking.

KATE I know, but why are you cooking now? It's three o'clock in the morning!

JAY I'm sorry, but I'm really hungry.

KATE Hmm . . . What are you making?

JAY Spaghetti.

KATE With tomato sauce?

JAY With tomato sauce and cheese.

KATE I love spaghetti! Uh . . . I'm getting hungry, too.

JAY Good. Let's eat!

6 PRONUNCIATION Rising and falling intonation

A Listen and practice. Notice the intonation of the yes/no and Wh-questions.

Is he cooking? ↗	What's he making? ↘
Are they sleeping?	What are they doing?

B Listen to the questions. Draw a rising arrow (↗) for rising intonation and a falling arrow (↘) for falling intonation.

1. ↗ **2.** ______ **3.** ______ **4.** ______ **5.** ______ **6.** ______

7 GRAMMAR FOCUS

Present continuous Wh-questions

San Diego 4:00 A.M.

What's Daniel **doing**?

He**'s sleeping** right now.

Guadalajara 6:00 A.M.

What's Leticia **doing**?

It's 6:00 A.M., so she**'s getting up**.

Washington, D.C. 7:00 A.M.

What are Lya and Erin **doing**?

They're having breakfast.

Brasilia 9:00 A.M.

What's Tiago **doing**?

He**'s going** to work.

Edinburgh noon

What are Kim and Paul **doing**?

It's noon, so they**'re eating** lunch.

Cairo 3:00 P.M.

What's Amina **doing**?

She**'s working**.

Jakarta 7:00 P.M.

What's Tamara **doing**?

She**'s eating** dinner right now.

Osaka 9:00 P.M.

What's Kento **doing**?

He**'s checking** his messages.

Your city 00:00

What are you **doing**?

It's . . . **I'm** . . .

GRAMMAR PLUS *see page 136*

A PAIR WORK Ask and answer the questions about the pictures.

1. Who's having breakfast?
2. Who's eating dinner?
3. Where's Amina working?
4. Where's Kento checking his messages?
5. What's Daniel doing?
6. What's Tiago wearing?
7. Why is Leticia getting up?
8. Why are Kim and Paul having lunch?

spelling

sleep → slee**ping**

get → get**ting** (+ t)

have → hav**ing** (– e)

B GROUP WORK Write five more questions about the pictures. Then ask and answer your questions in groups.

8 WORD POWER What are they doing?

A Listen and practice. *"They're dancing."*

dance

drive

listen to music

play basketball

read

ride a bike

run

shop

study

swim

take a walk

watch a movie

B **PAIR WORK** Ask and answer questions about the pictures in part A.

A: Are they running?
B: No, they're not.

A: What are they doing?
B: They're dancing.

C **GROUP WORK** Make two teams. Write an activity on a piece of paper. Give the paper to the other team. Two members act out each activity. Their team guesses. Can they guess the activity?

A: Are you running?
B: No, we're not.

C: Are you riding bikes?
D: Yes, we are!

9 INTERCHANGE 5 What's wrong with this picture?

What's wrong with this picture? Go to Interchange 5 on page 119.

10 READING

A Skim the conversation. Write the name of the correct person on each picture.

MESSAGE ME!

Eva and Pam are friends. They message on social media every day. Pam lives in Atlanta, in the United States. Eva is visiting friends in Puebla, Mexico.

Profile | Photos | Share | Find Friends

Eva35 Hey! How are you today, Pam?

PamL Hi, Eva! I'm fine, thanks. What are you doing?

Eva35 I'm sitting on the couch watching a movie. It's great!

PamL Lucky you! I'm writing a report. It's for my job.

Eva35 Oh, really? Are you at your office?

PamL Yeah. My friend Lety is making me coffee. She's helping me with the report.

Eva35 Cool. I'm . . . Oh, wait. My cell phone is ringing. Be right back. Sorry. It's my friend, Paul. He's making lunch.

PamL Right. I have to go, Eva. Sorry. My boss is calling me.

Eva35 OK. Good luck with the report! Have a good evening!

PamL Thanks, Eva. Enjoy your movie!

B Read the conversation. Who is doing these things? Choose the correct answers.

1. Pam	Eva	. . . is watching a movie.
2. Eva	Pam	. . . is visiting friends.
3. Pam	Eva	. . . is working in an office.
4. Lety	Paul	. . . is making coffee.
5. Paul	Pam	. . . is calling Eva on her cell phone.
6. Eva	Pam's boss	. . . is calling Pam.

C PAIR WORK Think about online conversations you have with friends. What do you say? What do you ask about? Write a short conversation.

6 I ride my bike to school.

- Discuss transportation and family
- Discuss daily and weekly routines

1 SNAPSHOT

Listen and practice.

Check (✓) the kinds of transportation you use.
What are some other kinds of transportation?

2 CONVERSATION They use public transportation.

Listen and practice.

Yuto: Nice car, Austin! Is it yours?

Austin: No, it's my sister's. She has a new job and she drives to work.

Yuto: Is her job here in the suburbs?

Austin: No, it's downtown.

Yuto: My parents work downtown, but they don't drive to work. They use public transportation.

Austin: The bus or the train?

Yuto: The bus doesn't stop near our house, so they take the train.

3 WORD POWER Family members

A PAIR WORK Complete the sentences about the Mitchell family. Then listen and check your answers.

1. Lisa is Tom's ___wife___.
2. Megan and Austin are their ______________.
3. Tom is Lisa's ______________.
4. Austin is Lisa's ______________.
5. Megan is Tom's ______________.
6. Austin is Megan's ______________.
7. Megan is Austin's ______________.
8. Tom and Lisa are Austin's ______________.

kids = children
mom = mother
dad = father

B PAIR WORK Who are the people in your family? What are their names?

"My father's name is Arthur. My sisters' names are Emilia and Sabrina."

4 GRAMMAR FOCUS

Simple present statements

I	**walk**	to school.	I	**don't live**	far from here.	**don't** = do not
You	**ride**	your bike to school.	You	**don't live**	near here.	**doesn't** = does not
He	**works**	near here.	He	**doesn't work**	downtown.	
She	**takes**	the bus to work.	She	**doesn't drive**	to work.	
We	**live**	with our parents.	We	**don't live**	alone.	
They	**use**	public transportation.	They	**don't need**	a car.	

GRAMMAR PLUS *see page 137*

A Tom Mitchell is talking about his family. Complete the sentences with the correct verb forms. Then compare with a partner.

1. My family and I ___live___ (live / lives) in the suburbs. My wife and I ______________ (work / works) near here, so we ______________ (walk / walks) to work. Our daughter Megan ______________ (work / works) downtown, so she ______________ (drive / drives) to work. Our son ______________ (don't / doesn't) drive. He ______________ (ride / rides) his bike to school.

2. My parents ______________ (live / lives) in the city. My mother ______________ (take / takes) the subway to work. My father is retired, so he ______________ (don't / doesn't) work now. He also ______________ (use / uses) public transportation, so they ______________ (don't / doesn't) need a car.

verb endings: *he, she, it*

walk → walk**s**
ride → ride**s**
study → stud**ies**
watch → watch**es**

Simple present statements with irregular verbs

I/you/we/they	*he/she/it*
I **have** a bike.	My mother **has** a car.
We **do** our homework every day.	My father **does** a lot of work at home.
My parents **go** to work by train.	The train **goes** downtown.

GRAMMAR PLUS *see page 137*

B Yuto is talking about his family and his friend Austin. Complete the sentences. Then compare with a partner.

1. My parents ___have___ (have / has) a house in the suburbs. My mom and dad ____________ (go / goes) downtown to work. My parents are very busy, so I ____________ (do / does) a lot of work at home.
2. My brother doesn't live with us. He ____________ (have / has) an apartment in the city. He ____________ (go / goes) to school all day, and he ____________ (do / does) his homework at night.
3. I ____________ (have / has) a new friend. His name is Austin. We ____________ (go / goes) to the same school, and sometimes we ____________ (do / does) our homework together.

C **PAIR WORK** Tell your partner about your family.

"I have one brother and two sisters. My brother is a teacher. He has a car, so he drives to work."

5 PRONUNCIATION Third-person singular –*s* endings

Listen and practice. Notice the pronunciation of the **–s** endings.

s = /s/		**s** = /z/		**(e)s** = /ɪz/		*irregular*	
take	tak**es**	drive	driv**es**	dance	danc**es**	do	do**es**
sleep	sleep**s**	study	studi**es**	watch	watch**es**	have	ha**s**

6 CONVERSATION What time do you get up?

Listen and practice.

Paige: Let's go to the park Sunday morning.

Adam: Good idea, but let's go in the afternoon. I sleep late on weekends.

Paige: What time do you get up?

Adam: I get up at noon.

Paige: Really? That's late. Do you eat breakfast at noon?

Adam: Yeah. What time do *you* get up?

Paige: At ten o'clock.

Adam: Oh, that's early for a Sunday.

Paige: Hey, I have an idea! Let's eat at Park Café. They serve breakfast all day!

7 GRAMMAR FOCUS

Simple present questions

Do you **get up** early on Sundays?	**What time do** you **get up**?
No, I **get up** late.	At noon.
Does he **eat** breakfast at seven o'clock?	**What time does** she have dinner?
No, he **eats** breakfast at seven-thirty.	At eight o'clock.
Do they **take** a taxi to class?	**When do** they **take** the subway?
No, they **take** the bus.	On Mondays and Wednesdays.

GRAMMAR PLUS *see page 137*

A Complete the questions with *do* or *does*.

1. *Do* you get up late on Sundays?
2. ______ you have lunch at home every day?
3. What time ______ your father leave work on Fridays?
4. ______ your mother cook on weekdays?
5. ______ your father shop on Saturdays?
6. ______ you take a walk in the evening?
7. When ______ you listen to music?
8. What time ______ you check your email?
9. What time ______ your parents have dinner?
10. When ______ you study English?
11. ______ your best friend ride a bike on weekends?
12. ______ your father drive to work every morning?

time expressions	
early	**in** the morning
late	**in** the afternoon
every day	**in** the evening
at 9:00	**on** Sundays
at noon/midnight	**on** weekdays
at night	**on** weekends

B PAIR WORK Ask and answer the questions from part A. Use time expressions from the box.

A: Do you get up late on Sundays?
B: No, I don't. I get up at eight o'clock. I play basketball on Sunday mornings.

C Unscramble the questions to complete the conversations. Then ask a partner the questions. Answer with your own information.

1. **A:** *What time do you eat dinner*?
   you / what time / dinner / do / eat
   B: At 7:00 P.M.
2. **A:** ______?
   you / every morning / check your messages / do
   B: Yes, I check my messages on the bus every morning.
3. **A:** ______?
   at / start / does / seven o'clock / this class
   B: No, this class starts at eight o'clock.
4. **A:** ______?
   listen to music / you / do / when
   B: I listen to music in the evening.
5. **A:** ______?
   on weekends / you and your friends / do / play sports
   B: Yes, we play volleyball on Saturdays.

8 LISTENING Kayla's weekly routine

Listen to Kayla talk about her weekly routine. Check (✓) the days she does each thing.

	Monday	Tuesday	Wednesday	Thursday	Friday	Saturday	Sunday
get up early	☐	☐	☐	☐	☐	☐	☐
go to work	☐	☐	☐	☐	☐	☐	☐
play tennis	☐	☐	☐	☐	☐	☐	☐
go shopping	☐	☐	☐	☐	☐	☐	☐
see friends	☐	☐	☐	☐	☐	☐	☐
dinner with family	☐	☐	☐	☐	☐	☐	☐
study	☐	☐	☐	☐	☐	☐	☐

9 SPEAKING My weekly routine

A What do you do every week? Write your routine in the chart.

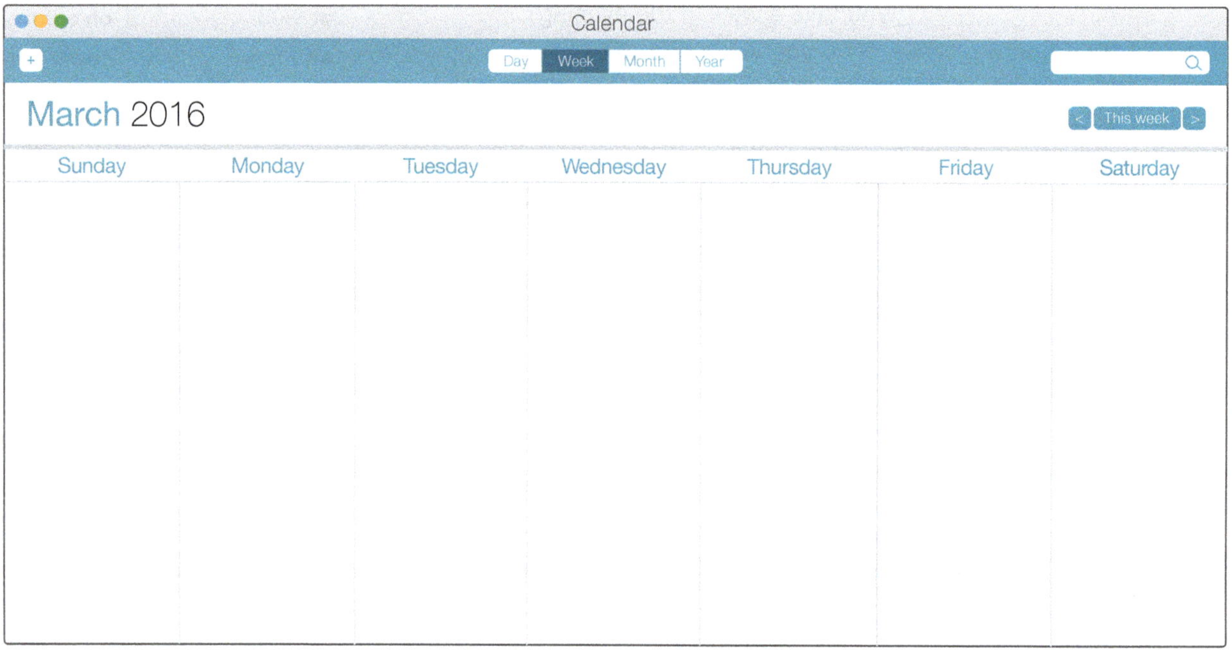

B GROUP WORK Discuss your weekly routines. Ask and answer questions.

A: I play tennis on Sunday mornings.
B: What do you do on Sunday afternoons?
A: I see my friends. We watch movies or play games. What about you?
C: On Sundays, I have lunch with my parents. In the afternoon, we talk or take a walk.

10 INTERCHANGE 6 Class survey

Find out more about your classmates.
Go to Interchange 6 on page 120.

11 READING

A Scan the interview. What's unusual about Mike's job?

What's your schedule like?

Every week, we interview someone with an unusual schedule. In this week's interview, we meet Mike Watts, a professional "sleeper." Yes, that's correct. Mike's job pays him to sleep! Here, Mike talks to us about his schedule.

News Now: Hi Mike, thanks for talking to us. What's your schedule like?

Mike: Hi there! My schedule's strange, but I love it. I go to bed at 10:00 P.M. in a different hotel room every night.

News Now: Wow! That's cool! Do you get up early?

Mike: Yes, I get up at 6:00 A.M. I'm an early bird! I like the morning. At 8:00 A.M., I have a big breakfast in the hotel restaurant.

News Now: So, who pays you to do that?

Mike: I work for a travel blog. They pay me to stay in different hotels and write about them. People read the blog and go to the hotels. Right now, I'm at a hotel in Finland, Hotel Finn.

News Now: And what do you do before you go to bed?

Mike: Every afternoon, from 2:00 P.M. to 4:00 P.M., I write about each room. I talk about the bed, the lights, the noise . . .

News Now: Who reads the blog?

Mike: Lots of different people read it. Business people, tourists, travel agencies . . . people who want to know about hotels, really!

News Now: What do you do in the evening?

Mike: At 7:00 P.M., I talk to the hotel manager. Then I go to my new room and go to bed.

News Now: Do you like sleeping?

Mike: Yes, I do! I'm very good at it!

B Read the article. Number the activities in Mike's schedule from 1 to 5. Then answer the questions. Write the times.

_____ **a.** Mike writes about each room.
__1__ **b.** He gets up.
_____ **c.** He talks to the hotel manager.
_____ **d.** He goes to his new room.
_____ **e.** He has a big breakfast.

1. What time does Mike write about each room? __________
2. What time does he get up? __________
3. What time does he talk to the hotel manager? __________
4. What time does he go to bed? __________
5. What time does he have breakfast? __________

C Are you an "early bird," like Mike? Or are you a "night owl"? Write five sentences about your schedule. Compare with a partner.

early bird

night owl

Units 5–6 Progress check

SELF-ASSESSMENT

How well can you do these things? Check (✓) the boxes.

I can . . .	Very well	OK	A little
Understand times and descriptions of activities (Ex. 1)	☐	☐	☐
Ask and answer questions about present activities (Ex. 2)	☐	☐	☐
Talk about personal routines (Ex. 3)	☐	☐	☐
Ask and answer questions about routines (Ex. 4)	☐	☐	☐
Ask and answer questions about celebrities' appearances and activities (Ex. 5)	☐	☐	☐

1 LISTENING I'm calling from Los Angeles.

It's 9:00 A.M. in Los Angeles. Stephanie is calling friends around the world. Listen to the conversations and complete the chart.

	1. Chelsea	2. Carlos	3. Nicholas
City	New York		
Time			
Activity			

2 SPEAKING We're on vacation!

Student A: Imagine your classmates are on vacation. Student B calls you. Ask questions about your classmates.

Student B: Imagine you are on vacation with your classmates. Call Student A. Answer Student A's questions about your classmates.

A: Hello?
B: Hi, it's . . . . I'm on vacation in . . .
A: In . . . ? Wow! What are you doing?
B: . . .
A: Who are you with?
B: . . .
A: What's he/she doing?
B: . . .
A: Well, have fun. Bye!

3 SPEAKING One day in my week

A Choose one day of the week and write it in the blank.
What do you do on this day? Complete the chart.

	Day:
In the morning	
In the afternoon	
In the evening	
At night	

B **PAIR WORK** Tell your partner about your routine on the day from part A.

A: On Saturdays, I exercise in the morning. I run in the park with my friends.
B: What time do you run?
A: We run at 9:00.

4 SPEAKING Lifestyle survey

A Answer the questions in the chart. Check (✓) Yes or No.

	Yes	No	Name
1. Do you live with your parents?	☐	☐	
2. Do both your parents work?	☐	☐	
3. Do you play video games at night?	☐	☐	
4. Do you eat dinner with your family?	☐	☐	
5. Do you stay at home on weekends?	☐	☐	
6. Do you work on Saturdays?	☐	☐	

B **CLASS ACTIVITY** Go around the class and find classmates with the same answers.
Write their names in the chart. Try to write a different name on each line.

5 SPEAKING Guess who!

GROUP WORK Think of a famous person. Your classmates ask yes/no questions to guess the person.

Is it a man? a woman?
Does he/she live in . . . ?
Is he/she a singer? an actor?

Does he/she speak English?
Does he/she play soccer? basketball?
Does he/she wear glasses?

WHAT'S NEXT?

Look at your Self-assessment again. Do you need to review anything?

7 Does it have a view?

- Describe houses and apartments
- Discuss furniture and dream homes

1 SNAPSHOT

Listen and practice.

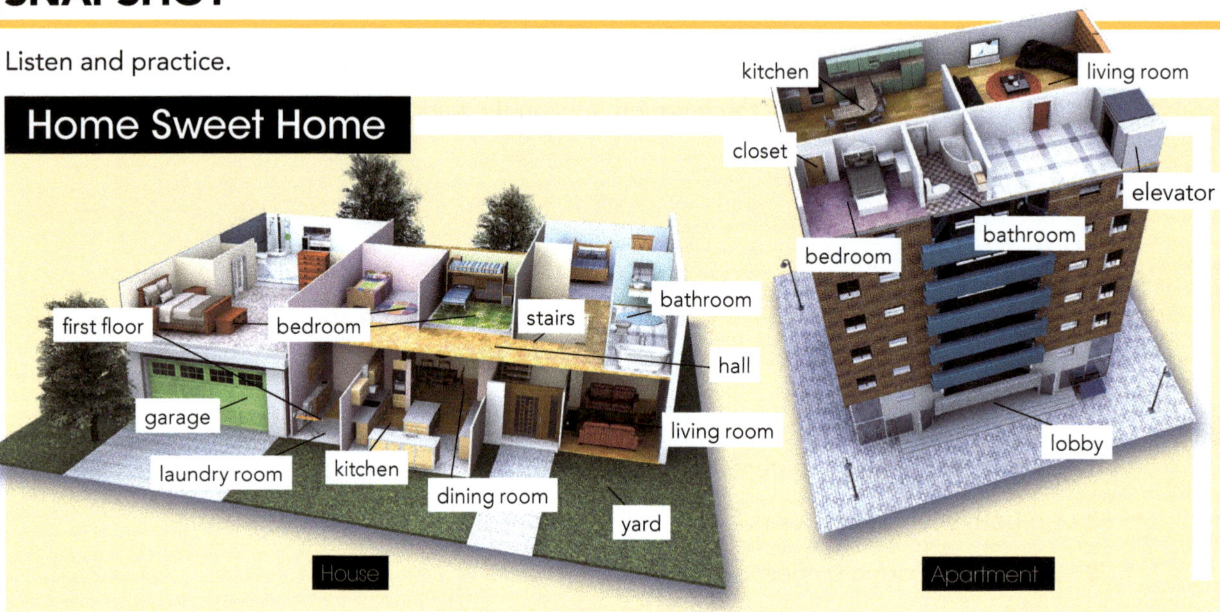

What rooms are in houses in your country? What rooms are in apartments?
What rooms are in your house or apartment? What is your favorite room?

2 CONVERSATION Do you live downtown?

Listen and practice.

Julia: Hi Ethan. Guess what! I have a new apartment.
Ethan: Hey! Cool! Do you live downtown?
Julia: No, I don't. I live near the university now.
Ethan: That's great! What's it like?
Julia: It's really nice. It has a big living room, a bedroom, a bathroom, and a kitchen.
Ethan: Awesome! Does it have an elevator?
Julia: Yes, it does.
Ethan: And does it have a nice view?
Julia: No, it doesn't. It has a view of another apartment building!

3 GRAMMAR FOCUS

Simple present short answers

Do you **live** in an apartment?	**Does** Ethan **live** in a house?
Yes, I **do**. / No, I **don't**.	Yes, he **does**. / No, he **doesn't**.
Do the bedrooms **have** closets?	**Does** the house **have** a yard?
Yes, they **do**. / No, they **don't**.	Yes, it **does**. / No, it **doesn't**.

GRAMMAR PLUS see page 138

A Complete the conversation. Then practice with a partner.

Julia ___Do___ you ___live___ in an apartment?
Ethan No, I ________. I ________ in a house.
Julia ________ it ________ a yard?
Ethan Yes, it ________.
Julia That sounds nice. ________ you ________ alone?
Ethan No, I ________. I ________ with my family.
Julia ________ you ________ any brothers or sisters?
Ethan Yes, I ________. I ________ four sisters.
Julia Really? ________ your house ________ many bedrooms?
Ethan Yes, it ________. It ________ four.
Julia ________ you ________ your own bedroom?
Ethan Yes, I ________. I'm really lucky.

B PAIR WORK Read the conversation in part A again. Ask and answer these questions about Ethan.

1. Does he live in an apartment?
2. Does his house have a yard?
3. Does he live alone?
4. Does he have his own room?

C PAIR WORK Write five questions to ask your partner about his or her home. Then ask and answer the questions.

4 LISTENING We have a nice yard.

Listen to four people describe their homes. Number the pictures from 1 to 4.

5 WORD POWER Furniture and appliances

A Listen and practice.

an armchair

a stove

curtains

pictures

a bed

a table

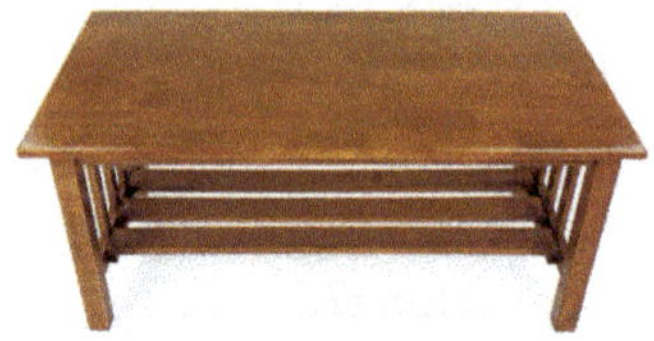
a coffee table

a microwave

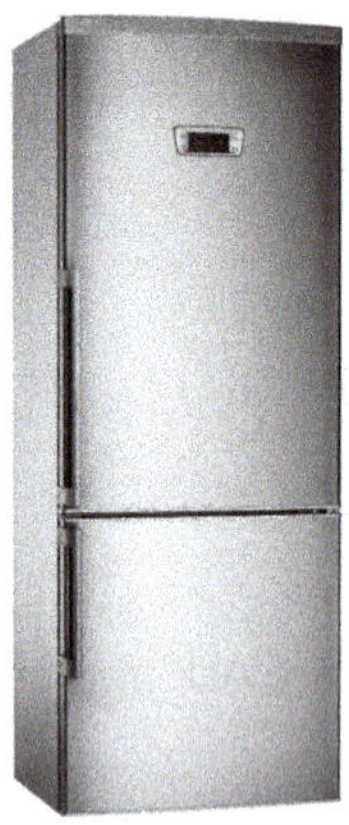
a refrigerator

lamps

a sofa

a desk

a coffee maker

a dresser

chairs

a mirror

a bookcase

a rug

cupboards

B Which rooms have the things in part A? Complete the chart.

A kitchen has . . .	a table a stove
A dining room has . . .	a table
A living room has . . .	
A bedroom has . . .	

C **GROUP WORK** What furniture is in your house or apartment? Tell your classmates.

"My living room has a sofa, a bookcase, and a rug . . ."

6 CONVERSATION I really need some furniture.

Listen and practice.

Eric: This apartment is great, Lara.

Lara: Thanks. I love it, but I really need some furniture.

Eric: What do you need?

Lara: Oh, lots of things. For example, there are some chairs in the kitchen, but there isn't a table.

Eric: That's true. And there's no sofa in the living room.

Lara: And there aren't any armchairs, there isn't a rug . . . There's only this lamp!

Eric: So let's go shopping next weekend!

7 GRAMMAR FOCUS

There is, there are

There's a bed in the bedroom.	**There are some** chairs in the kitchen.	There**'s** = There is
There's no sofa in the bedroom.	**There are no** chairs in the living room.	
There isn't a table in the kitchen.	**There aren't any** chairs in the living room.	

GRAMMAR PLUS *see page 138*

A Look at the picture of Ann's apartment. Complete the sentences. Then practice with a partner.

1. *There's no* dresser in the bedroom.
2. ______________ chairs in the kitchen.
3. ______________ lamp in the living room.
4. ______________ refrigerator.
5. ______________ rugs on the floor.
6. ______________ curtains on the windows.
7. ______________ armchair in the bedroom.
8. ______________ books in the bookcase.

B Write five sentences about things you have or don't have in your home. Then compare with a partner.

There are two sofas in my living room.

8 INTERCHANGE 7 Find the differences

Compare two apartments. Go to Interchange 7 on page 121.

9 PRONUNCIATION Words with *th*

A Listen and practice. Notice the pronunciation of /θ/ and /ð/.

/ð/ /θ/ /ð/ /ð/ /θ/ /θ/
There are **th**irteen rooms in **th**is house. **Th**e house has **th**ree ba**th**rooms.

B PAIR WORK List other words with /θ/ and /ð/. Then use them to write two sentences. Read them aloud.

There are thirty-three books on their bookcase.

10 LISTENING A furniture website

Listen to Jacob and Courtney talk about furniture on a website. What does Courtney like? What doesn't she like? Choose 🙂 (likes) or ☹ (doesn't like).

🙂 ☹ armchairs	🙂 ☹ a sofa
🙂 ☹ a rug	🙂 ☹ lamps
🙂 ☹ a bookcase	🙂 ☹ a mirror
🙂 ☹ a coffee table	🙂 ☹ curtains

11 SPEAKING My dream home

A Write a description of your dream home.

What is your dream home?
Where is it?
What rooms does it have?
What things are in the rooms?
Does it have a view?

My dream home is a loft in a big city. There is one large living room with a lot of windows. There are two bedrooms and . . .

B PAIR WORK Ask your partner about his or her dream home.

A: What is your dream home?
B: My dream home is a loft in a big city.
A: What rooms does it have?
B: Well, there is a big living room, a small kitchen . . .

a beach house

a loft in a big city

a country villa

a cabin in the mountains

12 READING

A Scan the article. Which hotel has a room that looks like a dessert?

TRAVELNEWS Home Posts Archives

Unique Hotels

Which do you like – the world of science or the world of fiction? In this week's vacation post, we discover a hotel made for fans of nature and another hotel for fans of stories.

Bubble Hotel, Allauch, France

4 new

Just imagine sleeping in a giant, clear bubble in a forest. That's exactly what happens here. At night, hotel guests lie in bed and watch the stars and moon. Each bubble has a comfortable bed and a nice bathroom with a shower. There's also an air-conditioner to keep the room cool in summer and a heater to keep it warm when it's cold outside.

Each bubble room is different. Guests choose the "Zen" bubble if they want to feel relaxed. Or they stay in the "Love Nature" bubble for a beautiful view. Sometimes there are rabbits and squirrels playing outside. Is there anything missing? Well, yes, there isn't a TV because no one needs a TV in a bubble!

The Roxbury, New York, the United States

4 new

In the mountains near New York City, there's a very unusual hotel. Its name is the Roxbury. It has many rooms, but every single room is different. There's the Wizard's Emeralds room, for example. It has a yellow "road" in the middle – just like in *The Wizard of Oz*. There's a green shower in the bathroom with big red flowers on the walls.

Do you like sweet things?
Maryann's Coconut Cream Pie room looks just like a dessert – good enough to eat! The bed is round like a pie, and the ceiling looks like whipped cream.

How about space?
When you walk into George's Spacepad, you see an enormous red bathtub. It glows in the dark! There isn't a shower, but there are silver curtains, crazy lights, and two cozy sofas. It's really out of this world!

B Read the article. What's in each hotel? Complete the sentences.

sofas	animals	moon	round bed	✓ yellow road
stars	bathtub	TV	shower	air-conditioner

At The Roxbury

1. In the Wizard's Emeralds room, there is a ___yellow road___.
2. There is a ________ in Maryann's Coconut Cream Pie room.
3. In George's Spacepad, there are two ________. There is a red ________, but there isn't a ________.

At the Bubble Hotel

4. There is a view of the ________ and the ________.
5. There is an ________ to keep the room cool.
6. There are sometimes ________ playing outside.
7. There isn't a ________.

C **GROUP WORK** Talk about these questions.

1. Which hotel do you like? Why?
2. Imagine you have a hotel. What do you do to make it interesting?

8 Where do you work?

- Discuss jobs and workplaces using simple present Wh-questions
- Discuss opinions about jobs using *be* + adjective and adjective + noun

1 WORD POWER Jobs

A Match the jobs with the pictures. Then listen and practice.

a. accountant	e. doctor	i. office manager	m. security guard
b. bellhop	f. front desk clerk	✓ j. police officer	n. server
c. cashier	g. host	k. receptionist	o. taxi driver
d. chef	h. nurse	l. salesperson	p. vendor

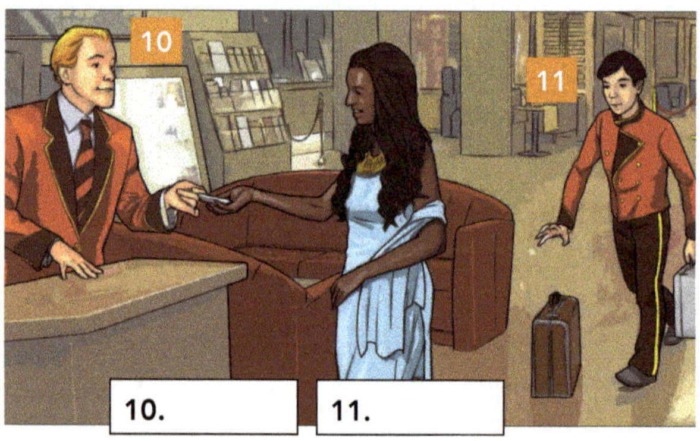

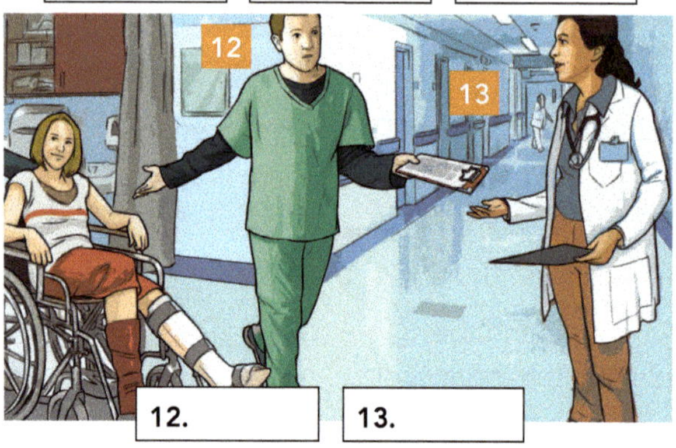

B PAIR WORK Ask questions about the people in part A. What are their jobs?

A: What does she do?

B: She's a police officer.

2 SPEAKING Workplaces

A PAIR WORK Who works in these places? Complete the chart with jobs from Exercise 1. Add one more job to each list.

A: A doctor works in a hospital. **B:** A nurse works in a hospital, too.

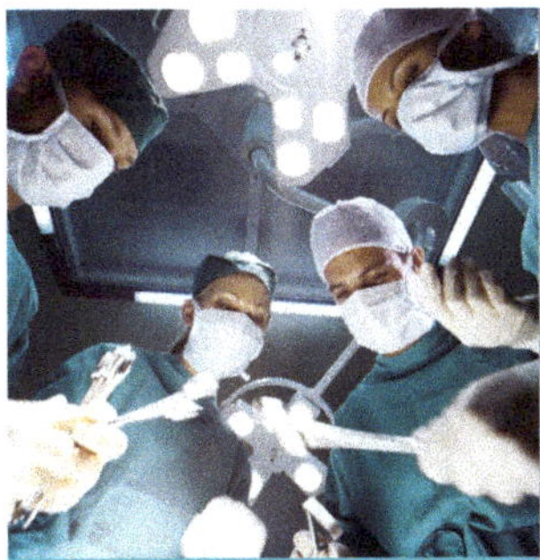

IN A HOSPITAL	IN AN OFFICE	IN A STORE	IN A HOTEL
a doctor			
a nurse			

B CLASS ACTIVITY Ask and answer *Who* questions about jobs. Use these words.

wears a uniform	sits all day	stands all day	works with a team
talks to people	works hard	works at night	makes a lot of money

A: Who wears a uniform?
B: A police officer wears a uniform.
C: A security guard wears a uniform, too.

3 CONVERSATION What does he do?

Listen and practice.

JORDAN Where does your brother work?
ALICIA In a hotel.
JORDAN Oh, really? My brother works in a hotel, too. He's an accountant.
ALICIA How does he like it?
JORDAN He hates it. He doesn't like the manager.
ALICIA That's too bad. What hotel does he work for?
JORDAN The Plaza.
ALICIA That's funny. My brother works there, too.
JORDAN Oh, that's interesting. What does he do?
ALICIA Actually, he's the manager!

4 GRAMMAR FOCUS

Simple present Wh-questions

Where do you **work**?	**Where does** he **work**?	**Where do** they **work**?
In a hospital.	In a hotel.	In an office.
What do you **do**?	**What does** he **do**?	**What do** they **do**?
I'm a doctor.	He's a manager.	They're accountants.
How do you **like** it?	**How does** he **like** it?	**How do** they **like** it?
I really like it.	It's OK.	They hate it.

GRAMMAR PLUS *see page 139*

A Complete these conversations. Then practice with a partner.

1. A: ___What___ does your sister ___do___?
B: My sister? She's a teacher.
A: _______ does she _______ it?
B: It's difficult, but she loves it.

2. A: _______ does your brother _______?
B: In an office. He's an accountant.
A: Oh? _______ does he _______ it?
B: He doesn't really like it.

3. A: _______ do your parents _______ their jobs?
B: Oh, I guess they like them.
A: I don't remember. _______ do they _______?
B: In a big hospital. They're doctors.

4. A: _______ do you _______?
B: I'm a student.
A: I see. _______ do you _______ your classes?
B: They're great. I like them a lot.

B **PAIR WORK** Ask questions about these people. Where do they work? What do they do? How do they like it?

Jeff

Jodie

Chad and Tracy

A: Where does Chad work?
B: He works in . . .

5 PRONUNCIATION Reduction of *do*

Listen and practice. Notice the reduction of **do**.

Where **do you** work? Where **do they** work?
What **do you** do? What **do they** do?

6 SNAPSHOT

Listen and practice.

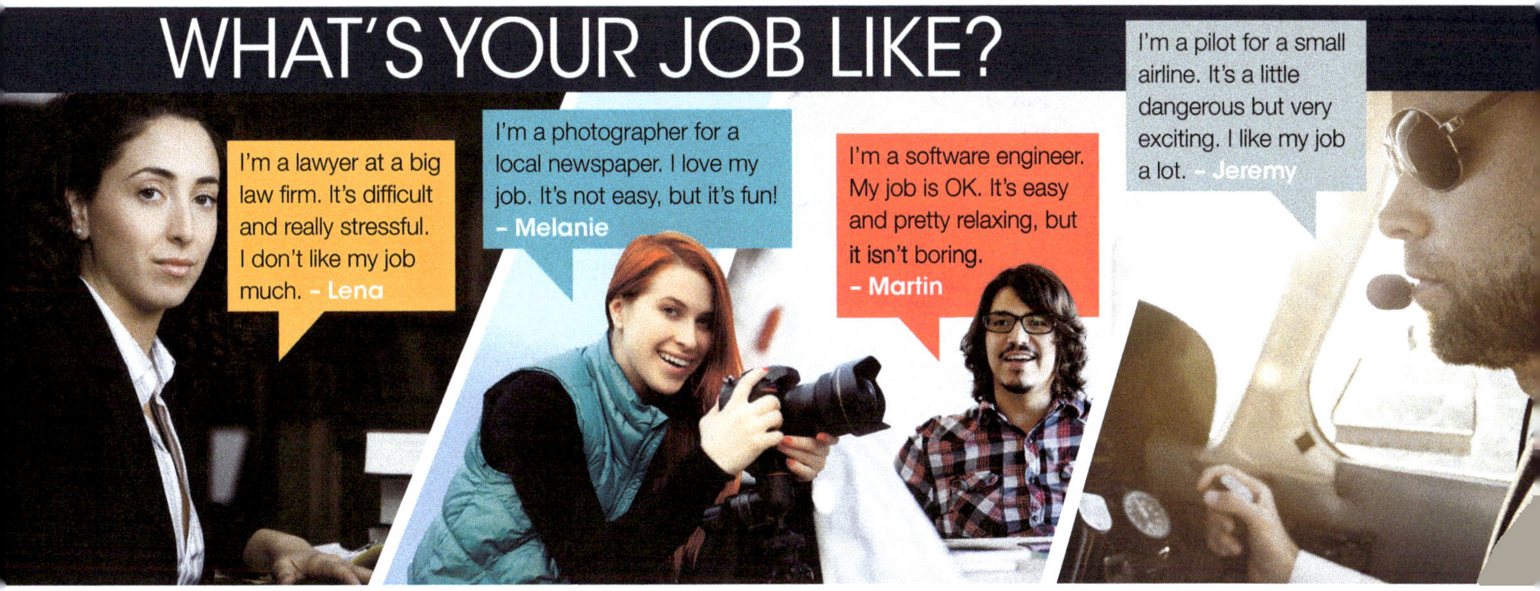

Who likes his or her job? Who doesn't? Why? Why not?
What jobs do you think are interesting? What jobs are not very interesting?

7 CONVERSATION It's a dangerous job.

Listen and practice.

JACK Hey, Paula. I hear you have a new job.

PAULA Yes. I'm teaching math at Lincoln High School.

JACK How do you like it?

PAULA It's difficult, but the students are terrific. How are things with you?

JACK Not bad. Guess what! I'm a firefighter now.

PAULA Really? Wow! How do you like it?

JACK It's a dangerous job, but it's really interesting. I love it!

PAULA OK, but please be careful!

8 LISTENING Is your job interesting?

Listen to four people talk about their jobs. Complete the chart with the correct jobs and adjectives.

	What do they do?	What's it like?
1. Yasmin		
2. Kana		
3. Luke		
4. Brandon		

9 GRAMMAR FOCUS

Placement of adjectives

***be* + adjective**	**adjective + noun**
A doctor's job **is stressful**.	A doctor has **a stressful job**.
A firefighter's job **is dangerous**.	A firefighter has **a dangerous job**.

GRAMMAR PLUS *see page 139*

A Write each sentence a different way. Then compare with a partner.

1. A photographer's job is interesting. *A photographer has an interesting job.*
2. A pilot's job is exciting. ______
3. A teacher's job is stressful. ______
4. A cashier has a boring job. ______
5. An accountant has a difficult job. ______
6. A receptionist has an easy job. ______

B GROUP WORK Write one job for each adjective. Do your classmates agree?

1. easy	*actor*	**4.** boring	______
2. difficult	______	**5.** exciting	______
3. dangerous	______	**6.** relaxing	______

A: A graphic designer has an easy job.
B: I don't agree. A graphic designer's job is difficult.
C: I think . . .

graphic designer

10 INTERCHANGE 8 The perfect job

What do you want in a job? Go to Interchange 8 on page 122.

11 SPEAKING Workday routines

GROUP WORK Ask three classmates about their jobs (or their friends' or family members' jobs). Then tell the class.

Ask about a classmate	Ask about a classmate's friend or family member
Do you have a job?	Tell me about your . . .
Where do you work?	Where does he/she work?
What do you do, exactly?	What does he/she do, exactly?
Is your job interesting?	Is his/her job difficult?
What time do you start work?	What time does he/she start work?
When do you finish work?	When does he/she finish work?
Do you like your job?	Does he/she like his/her job?
What do you do after work?	What does he/she do after work?

12 READING

A Do you think all jobs are boring? Think again! Look at the photos. What do these people do?

Home Posts Archives

Dream Jobs

Crocodile Researcher

I have a great job. I study crocodiles! It's an important job. Let me explain why. Here in Australia, we have a lot of crocodiles, but sometimes the crocodiles are sick. I want to know why. I study the food the crocodiles eat. I also learn how fast they grow and where they live. How do I do this? Well, in the morning, I take my camera, and I watch the crocodiles in the river. I take photos. Sometimes the crocodiles eat toads. Some toads make them sick and they die. I want to help the crocodiles.

Ice Cream Flavor Expert

Believe it or not, I taste ice cream for my job. Yes, it's a dream job, but it's also difficult! I work at a big ice cream company. Every day, I taste lots of different flavors three times each. Why is that? Well, I taste a little of the ice cream we make in the morning, afternoon, and at night. That way, I know that all the ice cream is good. I use my eyes first: Does the ice cream look nice? Then I taste the ice cream with a spoon: Does it taste fresh and sweet? Then I spit it out. Yes, I really spit it out!

Subscribe to our site

enter email Sign up

B Read the article. Check (✓) True or False.

	True	False
1. Both people have jobs they do outside.	☐	☐
2. The crocodile researcher studies what crocodiles eat.	☐	☐
3. The crocodile researcher watches the crocodiles at night.	☐	☐
4. The ice cream flavor expert tastes each flavor three times.	☐	☐
5. Ice cream flavor experts don't look at the ice cream.	☐	☐

C What's your dream job? Why? Write a short description. Compare with a partner.

Units 7–8 Progress check

SELF-ASSESSMENT

How well can you do these things? Check (✓) the boxes.

I can . . .	Very well	OK	A little
Ask and answer questions about living spaces (Ex. 1)	☐	☐	☐
Talk about rooms and furniture (Ex. 1)	☐	☐	☐
Ask and answer questions about work (Ex. 2)	☐	☐	☐
Understand descriptions of jobs (Ex. 3)	☐	☐	☐
Give and respond to opinions about jobs (Ex. 4)	☐	☐	☐

1 SPEAKING A new apartment

A Imagine you are moving into this apartment. What things are in the rooms? Draw pictures. Use the furniture in the box and your own ideas.

bed **chairs** **desk** **dresser** **lamp** **mirror** **sofa** **table**

B PAIR WORK Ask questions about your partner's apartment.

A: I'm moving into a new apartment!
B: That's great! Where is it?
A: . . .
B: What's it like? Does it have many rooms?
A: Well, it has . . .
B: Does the . . . have . . . ?
A: . . .
B: Do you have a lot of furniture?
A: Well, there's . . . in the . . .
There are some . . . in the . . .
B: Do you have everything you need for the apartment?
A: No, I don't. There's no . . .
There isn't any . . .
There aren't any . . .
B: OK. Let's go shopping this weekend!

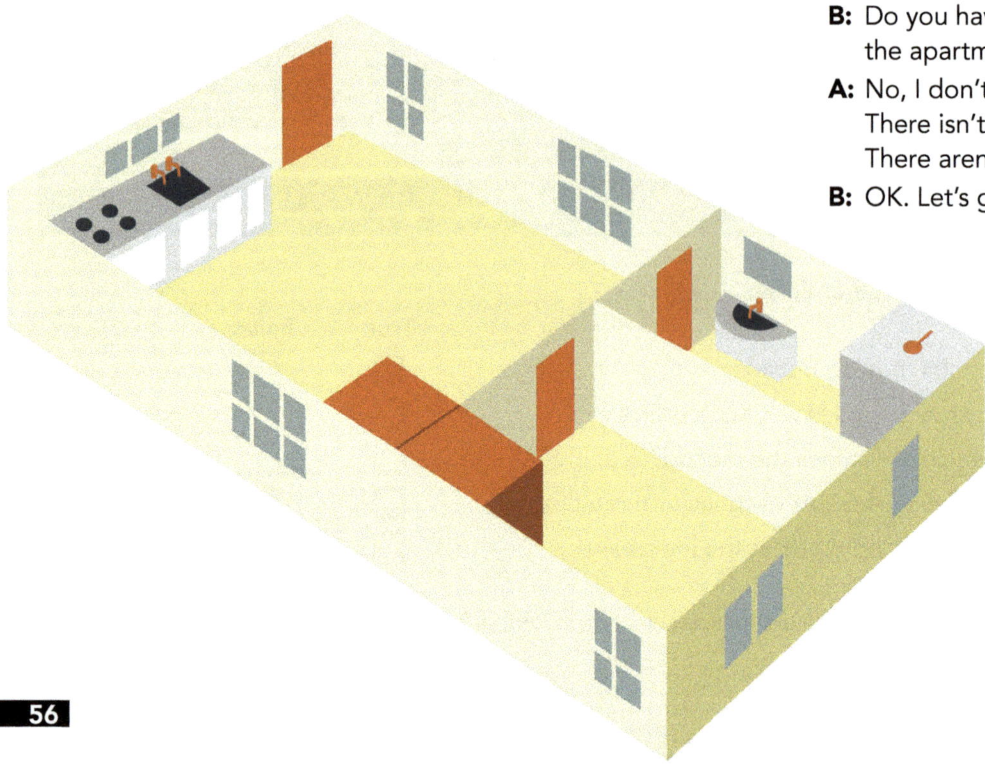

2 SPEAKING What does he do?

A Complete the conversations with Wh-questions.

1. **A:** *Where does your father work*?
   B: My father? He works in a store.
   A: ____________________?
   B: He's a salesperson.
   A: ____________________?
   B: He likes his job a lot!

2. **A:** ____________________?
   B: I'm an accountant.
   A: ____________________?
   B: I work in an office.
   A: ____________________?
   B: It's OK. I guess I like it.

B **PAIR WORK** Your partner asks the questions in part A. Answer with your own information.

3 LISTENING How do you like your job?

Listen to Rachel, Daniel, and Mai talk about their jobs. Check (✓) the correct answers.

	Where do they work?		What do they do?	
1. Rachel	☐ office	☐ store	☐ receptionist	☐ doctor
2. Daniel	☐ hospital	☐ school	☐ nurse	☐ teacher
3. Mai	☐ hotel	☐ office	☐ manager	☐ front desk clerk

4 SPEAKING Boring or interesting?

GROUP WORK What do you think of these jobs? Give your opinions.

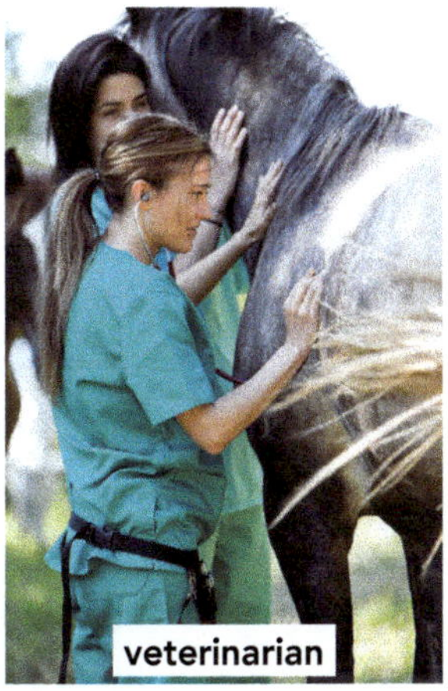

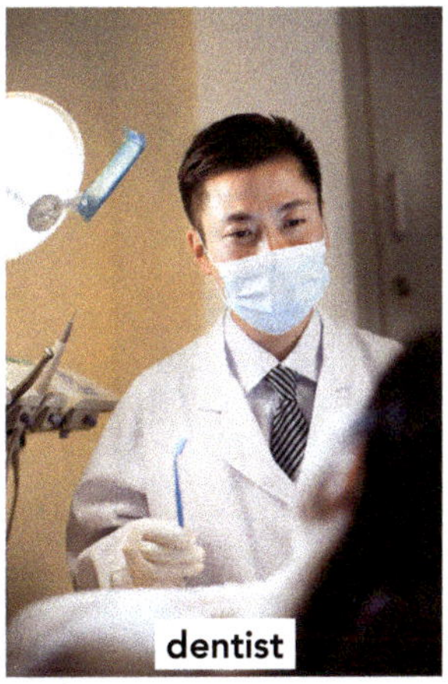

A: I think a veterinarian has a stressful job.
B: I don't really agree. I think a veterinarian's job is relaxing.
C: Well, I think a veterinarian's job is difficult. . . .

WHAT'S NEXT?

Look at your Self-assessment again. Do you need to review anything?

Interchange activities

INTERCHANGE 1 Celebrity classmates

A Imagine you are a celebrity. Write your name, phone number, and email address on the screens.

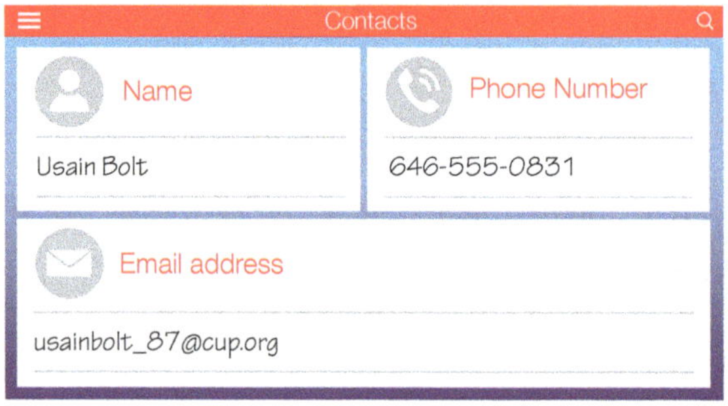

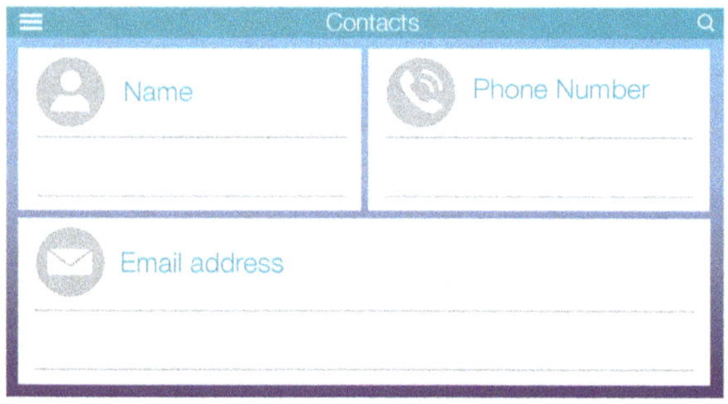

B **CLASS ACTIVITY** Go around the class. Introduce yourself to three "celebrities." Ask and answer questions to complete the screens.

A: Hi. My name is Emma Watson.
B: I'm Usain Bolt. Nice to meet you, Emma.
A: Usain, what's your email address?
B: It's U-S-A-I-N-B-O-L-T underscore eight-seven at C-U-P dot O-R-G.
A: I'm sorry. Can you repeat that?

useful expressions

I'm sorry.
Can you repeat that?
How do you spell that?

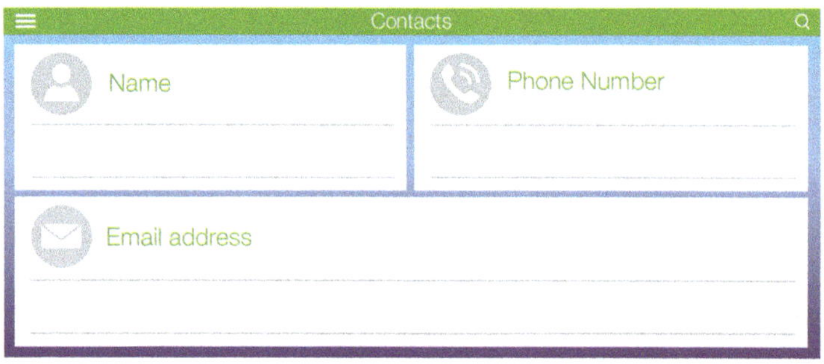

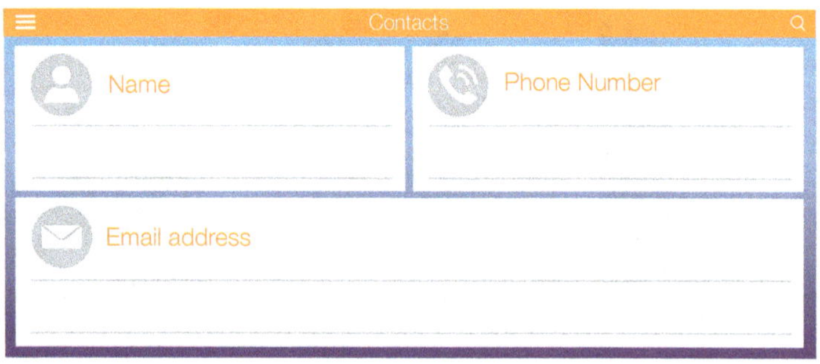

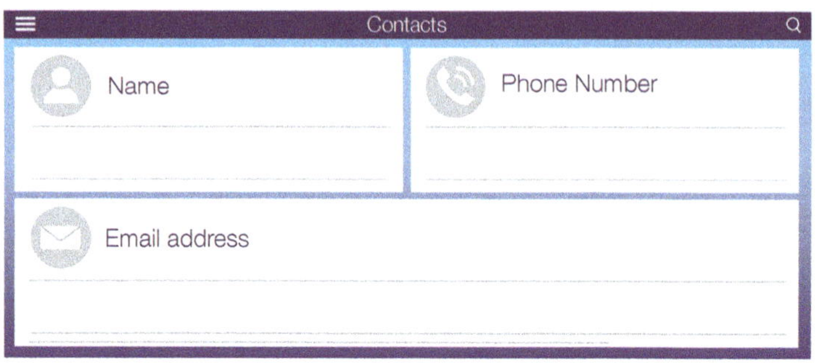

Emma Watson

Usain Bolt

INTERCHANGE 2 Find the differences

PAIR WORK How are the two pictures different? Ask questions to find the differences.

A: Where are the sunglasses?
B: In picture 1, they're on the bicycle.
A: In picture 2, they're on the table.

INTERCHANGE 4 Celebrity fashions

GROUP WORK Describe the people in the pictures. Don't say the person's name. Your classmates guess the person.

A: He's wearing blue jeans, a beige shirt, and a black jacket. Who is it?
B: Is it John Cho?
A: No, it isn't.
B: Is it Liam Hemsworth?
A: That's right.

Bradley Cooper

Rashida Jones

Neymar

Cristiano Ronaldo

Idris Elba

Scarlett Johansson

Ariana Grande

John Cho

Ang Lee

Kate Middleton

Zoe Saldana

Liam Hemsworth

INTERCHANGE 3 Let's talk!

A CLASS ACTIVITY Talk to your classmates. Ask two different classmates each question. Write their names and answers.

Question	Name:	Name:
What's your last name?		
Where are you from?		
What is your parents' first language?		
How do you spell your best friend's name?		
What's your best friend like?		
What is your email address?		
What is your phone number?		

B CLASS ACTIVITY Tell the class two things about your partners.

"Yumi's last name is Suzuki. Francisco is from Guatemala."

INTERCHANGE 5 What's wrong with this picture?

GROUP WORK What's wrong with this picture? Tell your classmates.

"Mia and Karen are playing basketball, but they're wearing dresses!"

INTERCHANGE 6 Class survey

A CLASS ACTIVITY Go around the class and find this information. Try to write a different name on each line.

Find someone who ...

Find someone who ...	Name
gets up at 5:00 A.M. on weekdays	
gets up at noon on Saturdays	
does homework on Sunday night	
works at night	
works on weekends	
has a pet	
dances on Friday night	
lives alone	
takes a bus to class	
rides a motorcycle to class	
cooks on weekends	
plays the drums	
has two brothers	
writes emails every day	
speaks three languages	
doesn't eat breakfast	

work at night

cook on the weekends

play the drums

A: Do you get up at 5:00 A.M. on weekdays, Kun-woo?
B: No, I get up at six-thirty.
A: Do you get up at 5:00 A.M. on weekdays, Yasmin?
C: Yes, I get up at 5:00 A.M. every day.

B GROUP WORK Compare your answers.

A: Kun-woo gets up at six-thirty on weekdays.
B: Yasmin gets up at 5:00 on weekdays.
C: Lucas gets up at . . .

INTERCHANGE 7 Find the differences

A **PAIR WORK** Find the differences between Tony's apartment and Nicole's apartment.

Tony's apartment

Nicole's apartment

A: There are four chairs in Tony's kitchen, but there are three chairs in Nicole's kitchen.
B: There is a sofa in Tony's living room, but there is no sofa in Nicole's living room.

B **GROUP WORK** Compare your answers.

INTERCHANGE 8 The perfect job

A **PAIR WORK** Imagine you're looking for a job. What do you want to do? First, check (✓) your answers to the questions. Then ask your partner the same questions.

	Me		My partner	
Do you want to . . . ?	**Yes**	**No**	**Yes**	**No**
work from 9 to 5	☐	☐	☐	☐
work in an office	☐	☐	☐	☐
work outdoors	☐	☐	☐	☐
work at home	☐	☐	☐	☐
work with a team	☐	☐	☐	☐
use a computer	☐	☐	☐	☐
use English	☐	☐	☐	☐
travel	☐	☐	☐	☐
talk to people	☐	☐	☐	☐
help people	☐	☐	☐	☐
wear a suit	☐	☐	☐	☐
perform in front of people	☐	☐	☐	☐

work from 9 to 5

perform in front of people

work outdoors

work with a team

Positive	Negative
It's easy. / It's an easy job.	It's difficult. / It's a difficult job.
It's exciting. / It's an exciting job.	It's boring. / It's a boring job.
It's terrific. / It's a terrific job.	It's very stressful. / It's a very stressful job.
It's pretty relaxing. / It's a pretty relaxing job.	It's really dangerous. / It's a really dangerous job.

B **PAIR WORK** Think of a good job for your partner. Go to pages 50 and 53 for ideas.

A: You want to travel and use English. Do you want to be a pilot?
B: No, a pilot's job is very stressful.
A: OK, do you want to be . . . ?

This page is intentionally left blank

Grammar plus

UNIT 1

1 *My, your, his, her* page 3

- Use *his* with males and *her* with females: **His** name is Travis. (NOT: ~~Her name is Travis~~.) **Her** name is Nicole. (NOT: ~~His name is Nicole~~.)

Complete the conversations with *my*, *your*, *his*, or *her*.

1. **A:** Hello. ___My___ name is Carlos.
   B: Hi, Carlos. What's __________ last name?
   A: It's Gonzales.
   B: How do you spell __________ last name? Is it G-O-N-Z-A-L-E-Z?
   A: No, it's G-O-N-Z-A-L-E-S. And what's __________ name?
   B: __________ name is Bill Powers. Nice to meet you.

2. **A:** What's Ms. Robinson's first name?
   B: __________ first name is Elizabeth. __________ nickname is Liz.
   A: I'm sorry. What's __________ first name again?
   B: It's Elizabeth. And what's Mr. Weber's first name?
   A: __________ first name is Peter.
   B: That's right. And __________ nickname is Pete.
   A: That's right, too!

2 The verb *be* page 5

- In questions, the verb *be* comes before the noun or pronoun: **Are you** Joshua Brown? **Is he** in our English class? **Is she** the teacher?
- Don't use contractions in short answers with *Yes*: Are you in my class? Yes, **I am**. (NOT: ~~Yes, I'm~~.)

Complete the conversations with the words in the box.

am	I'm	it's	she's	you're
✓ are	I am	I'm not	you	

1. **A:** Excuse me. ___Are___ you Layla Moore?
   B: No, __________. __________ over there.
   A: OK. Thanks.

2. **A:** Hi. Are __________ Layla Moore?
   B: Yes, __________.
   A: Nice to meet you. __________ Sergio Oliveira. __________ in my English class.
   B: Yes, I __________. __________ nice to meet you too, Sergio.

UNIT 2

1 *This/these; it/they*; plurals page 10

- Don't use a contraction with *What* + *are*: **What** are these? (NOT: ~~What're these?~~)
- Use *this* with singular nouns: **This** is a laptop. Use *these* with plural nouns: **These** are flash drives.

Choose the correct words.

1. **A: What's** / **What are** these?
   B: It's / **They're** my **flash drive** / **flash drives**.
2. **A**: **What's** / **What are** this?
   B: It's / **They're a** / **an** cell phone.
3. **A:** What's **this** / **these**?
   B: It's / **They're a** / **an** English book.

2 Yes/No and *where* questions with *be* page 11

- In questions with *where*, the verb comes after *Where*: **Where** is my credit card? (NOT: ~~Where my credit card is?~~) **Where** are my sunglasses? (NOT: ~~Where my sunglasses are?~~)

A Match the questions with the answers.

1. Is that your wallet? __c__
2. Are these your glasses? _____
3. Where are my keys? _____
4. Is this your bicycle? _____
5. Where's your tablet? _____

a. They're in your backpack.
b. No, it's not.
c. Oh, yes, it is!
d. It's on my desk.
e. No, they're not.

B Complete the conversation. Use the words in the box.

are they	it is	they are	where
it	it's	this	✓ where's

A: ___Where's___ my dictionary?
B: I don't know. Is ______________ in your backpack?
A: No, ______________ not.
B: Is ______________ your dictionary?
A: Yes, ______________ Thanks! Now, ______________ are my glasses?
B: ______________ on your desk?
A: Yes, ______________. Thank you!

UNIT 3

1 Negative statements and yes/no questions with *be*

page 17

- Use *be* + *not* to form negative statements: Ana **isn't** a student. (NOT: ~~Ana no is a student.~~)
- *You* is a singular and a plural pronoun: Are **you** from Rio? Yes, **I** am./Yes, **we** are.

A Unscramble the words to write negative statements.

1. is / of Canada / Toronto / the capital / not
   Toronto is not the capital of Canada.
2. Buenos Aires / not / from / we're
   ____
3. not / you and Ashley / in my class / are
   ____
4. is / my first language / Korean / not
   ____
5. from / my mother / not / is / Italy
   ____
6. my parents / not / are / they
   ____

B Complete the conversations.

1. **A:** ___Are___ you and your friend from Costa Rica?
   B: No, __________ not. __________ from the Dominican Republic.
2. **A:** __________ your first language Spanish?
   B: Yes, it __________. My parents __________ from Ecuador.
3. **A:** __________ Nadia and Rayan Lebanese?
   B: Yes, __________ are. But __________ in France now.
4. **A:** __________ my friends and I late?
   B: No, __________ not. __________ early!

2 Wh-questions with *be*

page 20

- Use *what* to ask about things. Use *where* to ask about places. Use *who* to ask about people. Use *What is/are . . . like?* to ask for a description.
- Use *how* to ask for a description: **How are** you today? Use how old to ask about age: **How old** is he?
- In answers about age, you can use only the number or the number + years old: He's **18**. OR He's **18 years old.** (NOT: ~~He has 18 years.~~)

Complete the questions with *how*, *what*, *where*, or *who*. Then match the questions with the answers.

1. _Who_ is that? _d_
2. ______ is her name? _____
3. ______ is she like? _____
4. ______ old is she? _____
5. ______ your family from? _____
6. ______ is Kyoto like? _____

a. We're from Japan – from Kyoto.
b. She's 18.
c. Her name is Hina.
d. She's my sister.
e. Oh, it's really beautiful.
f. She's very nice and friendly.

UNIT 4

1 Possessives page 24

- The noun comes after a possessive adjective: This is **my** T-shirt.
- Don't include the noun after a possessive pronoun: This T-shirt is **mine**.
- *Whose* can be used with singular and plural nouns: **Whose** scarf is this? **Whose** sneakers are these?

Complete the conversations. Use the words in the boxes. There are two extra words in each box.

his	mine	my	your	yours	✓ whose

1. **A:** ___Whose___ jacket is this? Is it ____________, Ethan?
   B: No, it's not ____________. Ask Matt. I think it's ____________.

her	my	mine	your	yours

2. **A:** These aren't ____________ gloves. Are they ____________?
   B: No, they're not ____________. Maybe they are Young-min's.

her	hers	their	theirs	whose

3. **A:** ____________ sweaters are these? Are they Rachel's?
   B: No, they're not ____________ sweaters. But these shorts are ____________.

2 Present continuous statements; conjunctions page 26

- The present continuous is the present of *be* + verb + *-ing*: It**'s raining**. She**'s wearing** a raincoat.
- The two negative contractions mean the same: **He's not/He isn't** wearing a coat.
  We're not/We aren't wearing gloves.

Change the affirmative sentences to negative sentences. Change the negative sentences to affirmative sentences.

1. Mr. and Mrs. Liu are wearing green caps. ___Mr. and Mrs. Liu aren't wearing green caps.___
2. It isn't snowing. ____________________
3. I'm wearing a winter coat. ____________________
4. You're wearing David's sunglasses. ____________________
5. Ayumi isn't wearing a scarf. ____________________

3 Present continuous yes/no questions; adjective + noun page 27

- In questions, the present continuous is *be* + subject + verb + *–ing*: **Is** it **raining**? **Are** you **wearing** a raincoat?
- Adjectives can come before nouns or after the verb *be*: He's wearing **a blue hat**. His hat **is blue**.
- Adjectives don't have a plural form: a **green hat**; two **green hats**.

Write questions using the words in parentheses. Then complete the responses.

1. **A.** ___Is Mr. Thomas wearing a dark blue coat?___ (wear, dark blue coat)
   B: No, he ____________.
2. **A:** ____________________ (wear, high heels)
   B: No, we ____________.
3. **A:** ____________________ (wear, a sweater)
   B: Yes, I ____________.
4. **A:** ____________________ (rain)
   B: Yes, it ____________.

UNIT 5

1 What time is it? / Is it A.M. or P.M.? page 31

- Remember: You can say times different ways: 1:15 = *one-fifteen* OR *a quarter after one.*

Write each sentence in a different way.

1. It's a quarter to four. *It's three forty-five.*
2. It's 7:00 P.M. *It's seven in the evening.*
3. It's six-fifteen. ______
4. It's 10 o'clock at night. ______
5. It's three-oh-five. ______
6. It's twenty-five to eleven. ______
7. It's one o'clock in the morning. ______
8. It's midnight. ______

2 Present continuous Wh-questions page 33

- Use the present continuous to talk about actions that are happening right now: What **are** you **doing**? **I'm talking** to you!
- In questions, the *be* verb comes after the question word: What **are you** doing?
- To form the continuous of verbs ending in *–e*, drop the *e* and add *–ing*: have → having.
- For verbs ending in vowel + consonant, double the consonant and add *–ing*: get → getting.

What are the people doing? Write conversations. Use the words in parentheses.

1. **A:** *What's Matt doing?* (Matt)
   B: *He's swimming.* (swim)
2. **A:** ______ (Jon and Megan)
   B: ______ (shop)
3. **A:** ______ (you)
   B: ______ (write a message)
4. **A:** ______ (Chris)
   B: ______ (cook dinner)

5: **A:** ______ (you and Tyler)
   B: ______ (watch a movie)

6: **A:** ______ (Sara)
   B: ______ (have pizza)

7. **A:** ______ (you and Joseph)
   B: ______ (study for the test)
8. **A:** ______ (Laura and Paulo)
   B: ______ (chat online)

UNIT 6

1 Simple present statements page 37 and Simple present statements with irregular verbs page 38

- In affirmative statements, verbs with *he/she/it* end in *–s*: He/She **walks** to school. BUT I/You/We/They **walk** to school.
- In negative statements, use doesn't with *he/she/it* and don't with all the others: He/She/It **doesn't** live here. I/You/We/They **don't** live here.
- Don't add *–s* to the verb: She **doesn't live** here. (NOT: ~~She doesn't lives here.~~)

Elena is talking about her family. Complete the sentences with the correct form of the verbs in parentheses.

My family and I ___live___ (live) in the city. We ____________ (have) an apartment on First Avenue. My sister ____________ (go) to school near our apartment, so she ____________ (walk) to school. My father ____________ (work) in the suburbs, so he ____________ (drive) to his job. My mother ____________ (use) public transportation – she ____________ (take) the bus to her office downtown. She ____________ (have) a new job, but she ____________ (not like) it very much. And me? Well, I ____________ (not work) far from our apartment, so I ____________ (not need) a car or public transportation. I ____________ (ride) my bike to work!

2 Simple present questions page 39

- In questions, use *does* with *he/she/it* and *do* with all the others: **Does** he/she/it get up early? **Do** I/you/we/they get up early?
- Don't add *–s* to the verb: Does she **live** alone? (NOT: ~~Does she lives alone?~~)

A Write questions to complete the conversations.

1. **A:** ___Do you use public transportation?___
   B: Yes, I use public transportation.
2. **A:** ______________________________
   B: No, my family doesn't eat dinner at 5:00.
3. **A:** ______________________________
   B: No, my brother doesn't take the bus to work.
4. **A:** ______________________________
   B: No, I don't get up late on weekends.

- Use *in* with *the morning/the afternoon/the evening*. Use *at* with *night*: I go to school **in** the afternoon and work **at** night.
- Use *at* with clock times: She gets up **at** 8:00.
- Use *on* with days: He sleeps late **on** weekends. She has class **on** Mondays.

B Complete the conversation with *at*, *in*, or *on*.

A: Does your family have breakfast together ___in___ the morning?

B: Well, we eat together ____________ weekends, but ____________ weekdays we're all busy. My parents go to work early – ____________ 6:30. But we eat dinner together ____________ the evening, and we have a big lunch together ____________ Sundays. We eat ____________ noon. Then ____________ the afternoon, we take a walk or go to the movies.

UNIT 7

1 Simple present short answers page 45

- Remember: I/You/We/They **do/don't**. He/She/It **does/doesn't**.

Choose the correct words.

A: **Do** / (**Does**) your family **live / lives** in an apartment?
B: No, we **don't / doesn't**. We **have / has** a house.
A: That's nice. **Do / Does** your house have two floors?
B: Yes, it **do / does**. It **have / has** four rooms on the first floor. And we **have / has** three bedrooms and a bathroom on the second floor.
A: And **do / does** you and your family **have / has** a yard?
B: Yes, we **do / does**. And how about you, Tim? **Do / Does** you **live / lives** in a house, too?
A: No, I **don't / doesn't**. My wife and I **have / has** a small apartment in the city.
B: Oh. **Do / Does** you **like / likes** the city?
A: Yes, I **do / does**. But my wife **don't / doesn't**.

2 *There is, there are* page 47

- Use *there is* with singular nouns: **There's** a bed. Use *there are* with plural nouns: **There are** two chairs.
- Use *some* in affirmative statements: There are **some** chairs in the kitchen. Use *any* in negative statements: There aren't **any** chairs in the bedroom.

Read the information about the Perez family's new house. Write sentences with the phrases in the box.

there's a	**there are some**
there's no	**there are no**
there isn't a	**there aren't any**

1. A living room? Yes.
2. A dining room? No.
3. A microwave in the kitchen? No.
4. A table in the kitchen? Yes.
5. Curtains on the windows? Yes.
6. Rugs on the floors? No.
7. Closets in the bedrooms? Yes.
8. Bookcases in the bedrooms? No.

1. *There's a living room.*
2. ______
3. ______
4. ______
5. ______
6. ______
7. ______
8. ______

UNIT 8

1 Simple present Wh-questions page 52

- Use *What* to ask about things: **What do** you do? Use *Where* to ask about places: **Where do** you work? Use *How do/does . . . like . . . ?* to ask for an opinion: **How does** he **like** his job?

Complete the conversations.

1. **A:** What does your husband do ______________________________?
   B: My husband? Oh, he's a nurse.
   A: Really? Where ______________________________?
   B: He works at Mercy Hospital.
2. **A:** Where ______________________________?
   B: I work in a restaurant.
   A: Nice! What ______________________________?
   B: I'm a chef.
3. **A:** How ______________________________?
   B: My job? I don't really like it very much.
   A: That's too bad. What ______________________________?
   B: I'm a cashier. I work at a clothing store.
4. **A:** What ______________________________?
   B: My brother is a doctor, and my sister is a lawyer.
   A: How ______________________________?
   B: They work very hard, but they love their jobs.

2 Placement of adjectives page 54

- Adjectives come after the verb *be*: A doctor's job **is stressful**. Adjectives come before nouns: A police officer has a **dangerous job**. (NOT: ~~A police officer has a job dangerous.~~)
- Adjectives have the same form with singular or plural nouns: Firefighters and police officers have stressful jobs. (NOT:. . . have ~~stressfuls~~ jobs.)

Use the information to write two sentences.

1. accountant / job / boring
   An accountant's job is boring.
   An accountant has a boring job.
2. salesperson / job / stressful
   ____
   ____
3. security guard / job / dangerous
   ____
   ____
4. actor / job / exciting
   ____
   ____
5. host / job / interesting
   ____
   ____
6. nurse / job / difficult
   ____
   ____

Grammar plus answer key

Unit 1

1 *My, your, his, her*

1. A: Hello. **My** name is Carlos.
   B: Hi, Carlos. What's **your** last name?
   A: It's Gonzales.
   B: How do you spell **your** last name? Is it G-O-N-Z-A-L-E-Z?
   A: No, it's G-O-N-Z-A-L-E-S. And what's **your** name?
   B: **My** name is Bill Powers. Nice to meet you.
2. A: What's Ms. Robinson's first name?
   B: **Her** first name is Elizabeth. **Her** nickname is Liz.
   A: I'm sorry. What's **her** first name again?
   B: It's Elizabeth. And what's Mr. Weber's first name?
   A: **His** first name is Peter.
   B: That's right. And **his** nickname is Pete.
   A: That's right, too!

2 The verb *be*

1. A: Excuse me. **Are** you Layla Moore?
   B: No, **I'm not**. **She's** over there.
   A: OK. Thanks.
2. A: Hi. Are **you** Layla Moore?
   B: Yes, **I am**.
   A: Nice to meet you. **I'm** Sergio Oliveira. **You're** in my English class.
   B: Yes, I **am**. **It's** nice to meet you too, Sergio.

Unit 2

1 *This/These; it/they;* plurals

1. A: **What are** these?
   B: **They're** my flash drives.
2. A: **What's** this?
   B: **It's** a cell phone.
3. A: What's **this**?
   B: **It's an** English book.

2 Yes/No and *where* questions with *be*

A

1. c 2. e 3. a 4. b 5. d

B

A: **Where's** my dictionary?
B: I don't know. Is **it** in your backpack?
A: No, **it's** not.
B: Is **this** your dictionary?
A: Yes, **it** is. Thanks! Now, where **are** my glasses?
B: **Are** they on your desk?
A: Yes, **they are**. Thank you!

Unit 3

1 Negative statements and yes/no questions with *be*

A

2. We're not from Buenos Aires.
3. You and Ashley are not in my class.
4. My first language is not Korean. / Korean is not my first language.
5. My mother is not from Italy.
6. They are not my parents.

B

1. B: No, **are** not. **We're/We are** from the Dominican Republic.
2. A: **Is** your first language Spanish?
   B: Yes, it **is**. My parents **are** from Ecuador.
3. A: **Are** Nadia and Rayan Lebanese?
   B: Yes, **they** are. But **they're/they are** in France now.
4. A: **Are** my friends and I late?
   B: No, **you're/you are** not. **You're/You are** early!

2 *Wh*-questions with *be*

2. **What** is her name? c
3. **What** is she like? f
4. **How** old is she? b
5. **Where** is your family from? a
6. **What** is Kyoto like? e

Unit 4

1 Possessives

1. A: **Whose** jacket is this? Is it **yours**, Ethan?
   B: No, it's not **mine**. Ask Matt. I think it's **his**.
2. A: These aren't **my** gloves. Are they **yours**?
   B: No, they're not **mine.** Maybe they are Young-min's.
3. A: **Whose** sweaters are these? Are they Rachel's?
   B: No, they're not **her** sweaters. But these shorts are **hers**.

2 Present continuous statements; conjunctions

2. It's snowing.
3. I'm not wearing a winter coat.
4. You're not/You aren't wearing David's sunglasses.
5. Ayumi is wearing a scarf.

3 Present continuous yes/no questions

1. B: No, **he's not/he isn't.**
2. A: **Are you wearing** high heels?
   B: No, **we're not/we aren't.**
3. A: **Are you wearing** a sweater?
   B: Yes, **I am**.
4. A: **Is it** raining?
   B: Yes, **it is.**

Unit 5

1 What time is it? / Is it A.M. or P.M.?

3. It's a quarter after six.
4. It's 10:00 P.M.
5. It's five (minutes) after three.
6. It's ten thirty-five.
7. It's one A.M.
8. It's 12:00 A.M./It's twelve (o'clock) at night.

2 Present continuous Wh-questions

2. A: What are Jon and Megan doing?
   B: They're shopping.
3. A: What are you doing?
   B: I'm writing a message.
4. A: What's Chris doing?
   B: He's cooking dinner.
5. A: What are you and Tyler doing?
   B: We're watching a movie.
6. A: What's Sara doing?
   B: She's having pizza.
7. A: What are you and Joseph doing?
   B: We're studying for a test.
8. A: What are Laura and Paulo doing?
   B: They're chatting online.

Unit 6

1 Simple present statements and Simple present statements with irregular verbs

My family and I **live** in the city. We **have** an apartment on First Avenue. My sister **goes** to school near our apartment, so she **walks** to school. My father **works** in the suburbs, so he **drives** to his job. My mother **uses** public transportation – she **takes** the bus to her office downtown. She **has** a new job, but she **doesn't like** it very much. And me? Well, I **don't work** far from our apartment, so I **don't need** a car or public transportation. I **ride** my bike to work!

2 Simple present questions

A

2. A: Does your family eat dinner at 5:00?
3. A: Does your brother take the bus to work?
4. A: Do you get up late on weekends?

B

B: Well, we eat together **on** weekends, but **on** weekdays we're all busy. My parents go to work early – **at** 6:30. But we eat dinner together **in** the evening, and we have a big lunch together **on** Sundays. We eat **at** noon. Then **in** the afternoon, we take a walk or go to the movies.

Unit 7

1 Simple present short answers

A: **Does** your family **live** in an apartment?
B: No, we **don't**. We **have** a house.
A: That's nice. **Does** your house have two floors?
B: Yes, it **does**. It **has** four rooms on the first floor. And we **have** three bedrooms and a bathroom on the second floor.
A: And **do** you and your family **have** a yard?
B: Yes, we **do**. And how about you, Tim? **Do** you **live** in a house, too?
A: No, I **don't**. My wife and I **have** a small apartment in the city.
B: Oh. **Do** you **like** the city?
A: Yes, I **do**. But my wife **doesn't**.

2 *There is, there are*

2. There's no / There isn't a dining room.
3. There's no / There isn't a microwave in the kitchen.
4. There's a table in the kitchen.
5. There are some curtains on the windows.
6. There are no / There aren't any rugs on the floors.
7. There are closets in the bedrooms.
8. There are no / There aren't any bookcases in the bedroom.

Unit 8

1 Simple present Wh-questions

1. A: Really? Where **does he work**?
2. A: Where **do you work**?
   B: I work in a restaurant.
   A: Nice! What **do you do**?
   B: I'm a chef.
3. A: How **do you like your job**?
   B: My job? I don't really like it very much.
   A: That's too bad. What **do you do**?
   B: I'm a cashier. I work at a clothing store.
4. A: What **do your brother and sister do**?
   B: My brother is a doctor, and my sister is a lawyer.
   A: How **do they like their jobs**?
   B: They work very hard, but they love their jobs.

2 Placement of adjectives

2. A salesperson's job is stressful.
   A salesperson has a stressful job.
3. A security guard's job is dangerous.
   A security guard has a dangerous job.
4. An actor's job is exciting.
   An actor has an exciting job.
5. A host's job is interesting.
   A host has an interesting job.
6. A nurse's job is difficult.
   A nurse has a difficult job.

Credits

The authors and publishers acknowledge the following sources of copyright material and are grateful for the permissions granted. While every effort has been made, it has not always been possible to identify the sources of all the material used, or to trace all copyright holders. If any omissions are brought to our notice, we will be happy to include the appropriate acknowledgements on reprinting and in the next update to the digital edition, as applicable.

Texts

The Roxbury for the adapted text on p. 49. Reproduced with kind permission; Attrap'Rêves for the adapted text on p. 49. Reproduced with kind permission.

Key: B = Below, BL = Below Left, BC = Below Centre, BR = Below Right, B/G = Background, C = Centre, CL = Centre Left, CR = Centre Right, Ex = Exercise, TC = Top Centre, T = Top, TL = Top Left, TR = Top Right.

Illustrations

337 Jon (KJA Artists): 24, 29, 85; **Mark Duffin**: 15, 12(T), 31(T), 44(T), 47, 115, 121; **Thomas Girard** (Good Illustration): 3, 11, 13, 23, 25, 36, 37, 50, 79(T), 89, 100, 102; **Dusan Lakicevic** (Beehive Illustration): 21, 41, 87; **Quino Marin** (The Organisation): 26, 31(B), 79(B); **Gavin Reece** (New Division): 27, 44(B), 45, 101; **Gary Venn** (Lemonade Illustration): 56, 88, 90, 91, 127, 128; **Paul Williams** (Sylvie Poggio Artists): 9, 30, 119.

Photos

Back cover (woman with whiteboard): Jenny Acheson/Stockbyte/GettyImages; Back cover (whiteboard): Nemida/GettyImages; Back cover (man using phone): Betsie Van Der Meer/Taxi/GettyImages; Back cover (woman smiling): PeopleImages.com/DigitalVision/GettyImages; Back cover (name tag): Tetra Images/GettyImages; Back cover (handshake): David Lees/Taxi/GettyImages; p. v: PhotoAlto/Sigrid Olsson/PhotoAlto Agency RF Collections/GettyImages; p. 2 (header), p. vi (unit 1): Paul Bradbury/OJO Images; p. 2 (CR): Paul Bradbury/Caiaimage/GettyImages; p. 2 (BL): Stefania D'Alessandro/WireImage/GettyImages; p. 2 (BR): Steve Granitz/WireImage/GettyImages; p. 4 (Ex 7.1): Maskot/Maskot/GettyImages; p. 4 (Ex 7.2): Design Pics/Ron Nickel/GettyImages; p. 4 (Ex 7.3): Dan Dalton/Caiaimage/GettyImages; p. 4 (Ex 7.4): Squaredpixels/E+/GettyImages; p. 5 (T): Fabrice LEROUGE/ONOKY/GettyImages; p. 5 (C): Erik Dreyer/The Image Bank/GettyImages; p. 5 (B): theboone/E+/GettyImages; p. 6: Maskot/Maskot/GettyImages; p. 7 (T): Peter Dazeley/Photographer's Choice/GettyImages; p. 7 (Ex 14.1): Tim Robberts/The Image Bank/GettyImages; p. 7 (Ex 14.2): Klaus Vedfelt/DigitalVision/GettyImages; p. 7 (Ex 14.3): Nicolas McComber/E+/GettyImages; p. 7 (Ex 14.4): Ariel Skelley/Blend Images/GettyImages; p. 8 (header), p. vi (unit 2): John Slater/Stockbyte/GettyImages; p. 8 (backpack): igor terekhov/iStock/GettyImagesPlus; p. 8 (cellphone): Peter Dazeley/Photographer's Choice/GettyImages; p. 8 (hairbrush): slobo/E+/GettyImages; p. 8 (sunglasses): Fodor90/iStock/GettyImages; p. 8 (wallet): bibikoff/E+/GettyImages; p. 8 (keys): Floortje/E+/GettyImages; p. 8 (umbrella): Picheat Suviyanond/iStock/GettyImages; p. 8 (energy bar): Juanmonino/iStock/Getty Images Plus/GettyImages; p. 8 (book): Image Source/Image Source/GettyImages; p. 8 (notebook): kyoshino/E+/GettyImages; p. 8 (pen): Ann Flanigan/EyeEm/Fuse/GettyImages; p. 8 (eraser): subjug/iStock/GettyImages; p. 8 (clock): GoodGnom/DigitalVision Vectors/GettyImages; p. 9 (tablet): daboost/iStock/Getty Images Plus/GettyImages; p. 9 (box): Guy Crittenden/Photographer's Choice/GettyImages; p. 9 (phone case): Jeffrey Coolidge/DigitalVision/GettyImages; p. 9 (television): Cobalt88/iStock/GettyImages; p. 9 (newspaper): -Oxford-/E+/GettyImages; p. 9 (Id): Daniel Ernst/iStock/Getty Images Plus/GettyImages; p. 9 (clip): Steven von Niederhausern/E+/GettyImages; p. 9 (ticket): Gediminas Zalgevicius/Hemera/GettyImages; p. 9 (purse): Stramyk/iStock/GettyImages; p. 10 (flash drive): zentilia/iStock/Getty Images Plus/GettyImages; p. 10 (laptop): Coprid/iStock/Getty Images Plus/GettyImages; p. 10 (laptops.): karandaev/iStock/GettyImages; p. 10 (keys): krungchingpixs/iStock/GettyImages; p. 10 (backpacks): pavila/iStock/GettyImages; p. 10 (umbrella): Kais Tolmats/E+/GettyImages; p. 10 (sunglasses): Zaharia_Bogdan/iStock/GettyImages; p. 10 (wallet): malerapaso/iStock/GettyImages; p. 10 (window): beright/iStock/GettyImages; p. 10 (credit card): freestylephoto/iStock/GettyImages; p. 10 (headphones): tiler84/iStock/GettyImages; p. 12 (backpack): JulNichols/E+/GettyImages; p. 12 (flash drive): Garsya/iStock/GettyImages; p. 12 (laptop): Creative Crop/Photodisc/GettyImages; p. 12 (newspaper): goir/iStock/GettyImages; p. 12 (computer): AlexLMX/iStock/GettyImages; p. 12 (chair): urfinguss/iStock/GettyImages; p. 12 (wallet): pioneer111/iStock/GettyImages; p. 12 (notebook): drpnncpp/iStock/GettyImages; p. 12 (tv): selensergen/iStock/GettyImages; p. 12 (glasses): bonetta/iStock/GettyImages; p. 15 (cellphone): Manuel Faba Ortega/iStock/GettyImages; p. 15 (cellphones): sunnycircle/iStock/GettyImages; p. 15 (purse): penguenstok/E+/GettyImages; p. 15 (purses): iulianvalentin/iStock/GettyImages; p. 15 (wallet): Nyo09/iStock/GettyImages; p. 15 (wallets): alarich/iStock/GettyImages; p. 16 (header), p. vi (unit 3): stock_colors/iStock/Getty Images Plus/GettyImages; p. 16 (T): Photography by ZhangXun/Moment/GettyImages; p. 16 (BL): Roberto Westbrook/Blend Images/GettyImages; p. 17 (T): Robert Frerck/The Image Bank/GettyImages; p. 17 (B): Jane Sweeney/The Image Bank/GettyImages; p. 18 (Ex 5.1): Dan MacMedan/WireImage/GettyImages; p. 18 (Ex 5.2): Steve Granitz/WireImage/GettyImages; p. 18 (Ex 5.3): Clasos/CON/LatinContent Editorial/GettyImages; p. 18 (Ex 5.4): Koki Nagahama/Getty Images AsiaPac/GettyImages; p. 18 (Ex 5.5): Jeff Spicer/Getty Images Entertainment/GettyImages; p. 19 (TR): SolStock/E+/GettyImages; p. 19 (cellphone): Peter Dazeley/Photographer's Choice/GettyImages; p. 19 (Ben): Hero Images/Hero Images/GettyImage; p. 19 (Nadia): Portra Images/DigitalVision/GettyImages; p. 19 (Ex 7.c.a): Fuse/Corbis/GettyImages; p. 19 (Ex 7.c.b): Purestock/GettyImages; p. 19 (Ex 7.c.c): Lucy Lambriex/Moment/GettyImages; p. 19 (Ex 7.c.d): James Woodson/Photodisc/GettyImages; p. 19 (Ex 7.c.e): Fuse/Corbis/GettyImages; p. 20 (Ex 8.a.1): Alex Barlow/Moment/GettyImages; p. 20 (Ex 8.a.2): Jupiterimages/Stockbyte/GettyImages; p. 20 (Ex 8.a.3): PhotoAlto/Frederic Cirou/PhotoAlto Agency RF Collections/GettyImages; p. 20 (Ex 8.a.4): Hill Street Studios/Blend Images/GettyImages; p. 22 (header), p. vi (unit 4): Sam Edwards/Caiaimage/GettyImages; p. 22 (formal man): Spiderstock/E+/GettyImages; p. 22 (formal woman): Grady Reese/E+/GettyImages; p. 22 (rain coat): EdnaM/iStock/Getty Images Plus/GettyImages; p. 22 (coat): DonNichols/E+/GettyImages; p. 22 (dress): ARSELA/E+/GettyImages; p. 22 (casual woman): BLOOM image/BLOOMimage/GettyImages; p. 22 (pajamas): madtwinsis/E+/GettyImages; p. 22 (swimwear): dendong/iStock/Getty Images Plus/GettyImages; p. 22 (shorts): 487387674/iStock/Getty Images Plus/GettyImages; p. 22 (cap): Steve Zmina/DigitalVision Vectors/GettyImages; p. 25 (brazilian flag): Image Source/Image Source/GettyImages; p. 25 (japanese flag): Jim Ballard/Photographer's Choice/GettyImages; p. 25 (american flag): NirdalArt/iStock/GettyImages; p. 25 (canadian flag): Encyclopaedia Britannica/UIG/Universal Images Group/GettyImages; p. 25 (TL): Andrea Pistolesi/Photolibrary/GettyImages; p. 25 (TR): Photograph by Kangheewan/Moment Open/GettyImages; p. 25 (BL): Bruce Leighty/Photolibrary/GettyImages; p. 25 (BR): EschCollection/Photonica/GettyImages; p. 25 (thermometer): Burke/Triolo Productions/Stockbyte/GettyImages; p. 29: PeopleImages.com/DigitalVision/GettyImages; p. 30 (header), p. vi (unit 5): Driendl Group/Photographer's Choice/GettyImages; p. 30 (Brian): Daniel Grill/GettyImages; p. 30 (Amar): Peter Cade/The Image Bank/GettyImages; p. 31 (Ex 3.a.1): Raimund Koch/The Image Bank/GettyImages; p. 31 (Ex 3.a.2): Science Photo Library/Science Photo Library/GettyImages; p. 31 (Ex 3.a.3): Paul Bricknell/Dorling Kindersley/GettyImages; p. 31 (Ex 3.a.4): SergeiKorolko/iStock/GettyImages; p. 31 (Ex 3.a.5): pagadesign/iStock/GettyImages; p. 31 (Ex 3.a.6): scanrail/iStock/GettyImages; p. 32 (T): Plume Creative/DigitalVision/GettyImages; p. 32 (BR): B. Sporrer/J.Skowronek/StockFood Creative/GettyImages; p. 32 (Jay): B. Sporrer/J.Skowronek/StockFood Creative/GettyImages; p. 32 (Kate): Rafael Elias/Moment Open/GettyImages; p. 33 (TL): Tetra Images/Brand X Pictures/GettyImages; p. 33 (TC): Hola Images/GettyImages; p. 33 (TR): Tim Robberts/The Image Bank; p. 33 (CL): annebaek/iStock/Getty Images Plus/GettyImages; p. 33 (C): Stockbyte/Stockbyte/GettyImages; p. 33 (CR): Caiaimage/Tom Merton/Caiaimage/GettyImages; p. 33 (BL): LWA/Sharie Kennedy/Blend Images/GettyImages; p. 33 (BC): sot/DigitalVision/GettyImages; p. 33 (BR): David Crunelle/EyeEm/EyeEm/GettyImages; p. 34 (dance): Blend Images - Ariel Skelley/GettyImages; p. 34 (drive): Westend61/Westend61/GettyImages; p. 34 (music): Hero Images/Hero Images/GettyImages; p. 34 (basketball): Daniel Grill/Tetra images/GettyImages; p. 34 (read): Peathegee Inc/Blend Images/GettyImages; p. 34 (bycycle): Daniel Milchev/The Image Bank/GettyImages; p. 34 (run): Ty Milford/Aurora Open/GettyImages; p. 34 (shop): BJI/Blue Jean Images/blue jean images/GettyImages; p. 34 (study): JAG IMAGES/DigitalVision/GettyImages; p. 34 (swim): J J D/Cultura/GettyImages; p. 34 (walk): Dougal Waters/Photographer's Choice RF/GettyImages; p. 34 (movie): Blend Images/Andres Rodriguez/Blend Images/GettyImages; p. 35 (Eva35): Sebastian Doerken/fStop/GettyImages; p. 35 (PamL): Denis Schneider/EyeEm/EyeEm/GettyImages; p. 35 (TL): Hero Images/Hero Images/GettyImages; p. 35 (BR): Betsie Van Der Meer/Taxi/GettyImages; p. 36 (header), p. vi (unit 6): Enrique Díaz/7cero/Moment/GettyImages; p. 36 (Ex 1.1): Image Source/DigitalVision/GettyImages; p. 36 (Ex 1.2): Kentaroo Tryman/Maskot/GettyImages; p. 36 (Ex 1.3): Susanne Kronholm/Johner Images Royalty-Free/GettyImages; p. 36 (Ex 1.4): Eternity in an Instant/The Image Bank/GettyImages; p. 36 (Ex 1.5): Marilyn Nieves/iStock/GettyImages; p. 36 (Ex 1.6): Matt Dutile/Image Source/GettyImages; p. 36 (Ex 1.7): Ciaran Griffin/Stockbyte/GettyImages; p. 36 (Ex 1.8): Maria Teijeiro/DigitalVision/GettyImages; p. 38: Robert Daly/Caiaimage/GettyImages; p. 39: Michael Berman/DigitalVision/GettyImages; p. 40: Frank van Delft/Cultura/GettyImages; p. 41: vadimguzhva/iStock/GettyImages; p. 42 (man): James Whitaker/DigitalVision/GettyImages; p. 42 (woman): Tyler Stableford/The Image Bank/GettyImage; p. 43: Pingebat/DigitalVision Vectors; p. 44 (header), p. vi (unit 7): Peter Adams/Photolibrary; p. 45 (lobby): piovesempre/iStock/GettyImages; p. 45 (apartment): Joe_Potato/iStock/GettyImages; p. 45 (house): Ron Evans/Photolibrary/GettyImages; p. 45 (kitchen): ttatty/iStock/GettyImages; p. 46 (armchair): xiaoke ma/E+/GettyImages; p. 46 (stove): taist/iStock/GettyImages; p. 46 (curtains): darksite/iStock/GettyImages; p. 46 (pictures): Glow Decor/Glow/GettyImages; p. 46 (bed): Emevil/iStock/GettyImages; p. 46 (coffee maker): GeorgePeters/E+/GettyImages; p. 46 (table): EdnaM/iStock/GettyImages; p. 46 (coffee table): DonNichols/E+/GettyImages; p. 46 (oven): mbbirdy/E+/GettyImages; p. 46 (refrigerator): JazzIRT/E+/GettyImages; p. 46 (lamps1): Creative Crop/DigitalVision/GettyImages; p. 46 (lamps2): stuartbur/E+/GettyImages; p. 46 (sofa): AnnaDavy/iStock/GettyImages; p. 46 (desk): Hemera Technologies/PhotoObjects.net/GettyImages; p. 46 (bookcase): DonNichols/iStock/GettyImages; p. 46 (dresser): Hemera Technologies/PhotoObjects.net/GettyImages; p. 46 (chairs): Firmafotografen/iStock/Getty Images Plus/GettyImages; p. 46 (mirror): Omer Yurdakul Gundogdu/E+/GettyImages; p. 46 (rug): DEA/G. CIGOLINI/De Agostini Picture Library/GettyImages; p. 46 (cupboards): ChoochartSansong/iStock/GettyImages; p. 47: Marco Baass/GettyImages; p. 48 (loft): Martin Barraud/OJO Images/GettyImages; p. 48 (mountains): Barrett & MacKay/All Canada Photos/GettyImages; p. 48 (villa): Maremagnum/Photolibrary/GettyImages; p. 48 (beach house): catnap72/E+/GettyImages; p. 49 (T): BERTHIER Emmanuel/hemis.fr/hemis.fr/GettyImages; p. 49 (B): Michael Marquand/Lonely Planet Images/GettyImages; p. 50 (header), p. vi (unit 8): iStock/Getty Images Plus/GettyImages; p. 51 (hospital): Vincent Hazat/PhotoAlto Agency RF Collections/GettyImages; p. 51 (office): PeopleImages/E+/GettyImages; p. 51 (store): Maskot/Maskot/GettyImages; p. 51 (hotel): DAJ/amana images/GettyImages; p. 51 (BR): Nevena1987/iStock/GettyImages; p. 51 (Jorden): Sam Edwards/OJO Images/GettyImages; p. 51 (Alicia): Philipp Nemenz/Cultura/GettyImages; p. 52 (BL): Digital Vision./DigitalVision/GettyImages; p. 52 (BC): PeopleImages/DigitalVision/GettyImages; p. 52 (BR): Glow Images, Inc/Glow/GettyImages; p. 53 (lawyer): rubberball/GettyImages; p. 53 (pilot): Katja Kircher/Maskot/GettyImages; p. 53 (photographer): stock_colors/E+/GettyImages; p. 53 (engineer): Thomas Barwick/Iconica/GettyImages; p. 53 (BR): Rubberball/Mike Kemp/Brand X Pictures/GettyImages; p. 53 (Paula): Marc Romanelli/Blend Images/GettyImages; p. 54 (T): Hero Images/Hero Images/GettyImages; p. 54 (B): Jetta Productions/Stone/GettyImages; p. 55 (B): Australian Scenics/Photolibrary/GettyImages; p. 55 (T): Eugenio Marongiu/Cultura/GettyImages; p. 57 (veterinarian): fotoedu/iStock/GettyImages; p. 57 (dentist): XiXinXing/XiXinXing/GettyImages; p. 57 (architect): John Lund/Marc Romanelli/Blend Images/GettyImages; p. 57 (hairstylst): Glow Images, Inc/Glow/GettyImages; p. 114 (CR): Pascal Le Segretain/Getty Images Entertainment/GettyImages; p. 114 (BR): Amanda Edwards/WireImage/GettyImages; p. 116 (Bradley Cooper): Steve Granitz/WireImage/GettyImages; p. 116 (Rashida Jones): Stefanie Keenan/WireImage/GettyImages; p. 116 (Neymar): David Ramos/Getty Images; p. 116 (Ronaldo): Anthony Harvey/Getty Images Entertainment/GettyImages; p. 116 (Idris Elba): Dave J Hogan/Getty Images Entertainment/GettyImages; p. 116 (Scarlett Johansson): Ray Tamarra/WireImage/GettyImages; p. 117 (Ariana Grande): Christopher Polk/Getty Images Entertainment/GettyImages; p. 117 (John Cho): John M. Heller/Getty Images Entertainment/GettyImages; p. 117 (Ang Lee): Pascal Le Segretain/Getty Images Entertainment/GettyImages; p. 117 (Kate Middleton): Anwar Hussein/WireImage/GettyImages; p. 117 (Zoe Saldana): Jon Kopaloff/FilmMagic/GettyImages; p. 117 (Liam Hemsworth): Joe Scarnici/Getty Images Entertainment/GettyImages; p. 118: PeopleImages.com/DigitalVision/GettyImages; p. 120 (TR): Garry Wade/The Image Bank/GettyImages; p. 120 (CR): Indeed/ABSODELS/GettyImages; p. 120 (BR): Joos Mind/Photographer's Choice/GettyImages; p. 122 (CR): urbancow/iStock/GettyImages; p. 122 (TR): George Doyle/Stockbyte/GettyImages; p. 122 (BL): Dennis K. Johnson/Lonely Planet Images/GettyImages; p. 122 (BR): baona/E+/GettyImages